PRAISE FOR *CHASING MISSION FIT*

"Higher education has been chasing mission fit for years, and the challenge for admissions professionals to find best-fit students has never been greater. Bart Caylor astutely describes modern enrollment challenges and offers practical insight into how institutions of all types can tell their unique story. Caylor's marketing expertise, years of experience, and knowledge of higher education are all on full display; however, the most compelling aspect of Caylor's work is his emphasis on mission and its impact on prospective students. It is the seminal idea of the book and his professional service. Every college and university would benefit from this useful and informative resource."

—Phil Cook, PhD, President, North American Coalition for
Christian Admissions Professionals (NACCAP)

"*Chasing Mission Fit* emerges as essential reading for leaders within Christian higher education. Bart Caylor, a seasoned expert in marketing and recruitment, draws upon a wealth of lifetime experiences to offer valuable insights. This book adeptly navigates the intricacies of identifying challenges and presents thoughtful solutions to address the significant complexities facing marketing and recruitment leaders in Christian higher education."

—Philip E. Dearborn, President, Association for
Biblical Higher Education

"*Chasing Mission Fit*, steeped in practical wisdom, reassures higher ed marketers that impactful marketing is not solely the domain of those with lavish budgets or extensive resources. In today's landscape, where higher education grapples with ever-shifting challenges, this guide illuminates the route to effective marketing strategies for schools big and small."

—Jaime Hunt, Vice President and Chief Marketing Officer, and Host of Confessions of a Higher Ed CMO

"This is absolutely the best book on enrollment marketing for Christian colleges I've seen in over 30 years of leadership in Christian higher education. Bart shares powerful and essential principles that dispel myths about college marketing. It's a very readable marketing manual, and the actions he outlines are both doable and will produce solid results. Obviously, there's no substitute for the basics of college recruiting - and it's hard work. But this book will be an invaluable guide for developing the right strategy and tools. I wish every enrollment leader across biblical higher education would thoroughly digest the wisdom Bart has shared and prove its truth with growing enrollment. I am so pleased to recommend this book with my highest commendation."

—David Medders, Executive Vice President, Association for Biblical Higher Education

"In *Chasing Mission Fit*, Bart Caylor takes the reins of higher education marketing, steering readers through a compelling journey toward excellence in student recruitment. As a prominent influencer in higher education marketing, Caylor articulates the need for differentiation and provides a pragmatic blueprint for administrators in 12 insightful chapters.

Caylor's brilliance shines through in his ability to speak directly to the intended audience – higher ed administrators, particularly those engaged in student recruiting, marketing, and public relations. Unlike some industry influencers who might leave readers feeling overwhelmed, Caylor strikes a perfect balance, ensuring his message is accessible and profound. This book is not just a manual; it's a conversation with someone deeply passionate about their work.

The twelve chapters unfold seamlessly, offering clear and concise counsel that empowers administrators to navigate the complex landscape of enrollment marketing. Caylor's wisdom is not theoretical; it's grounded in practical strategies that can be implemented immediately. The author's passion for the subject matter resonates throughout the book, creating an engaging and motivating experience for the reader.

Chasing Mission Fit is a testament to Caylor's mastery of higher ed marketing and marks a stellar debut for the author. The book is not merely a theoretical exploration but a hands-on guide, making it an invaluable resource for those looking to enhance their student recruiting and marketing capabilities.

The title rightfully earns its place not on the bookshelf but on the busy desk of every professional in higher education seeking to elevate their student recruitment efforts. Bart Caylor deserves applause for delivering a book that not only meets but exceeds the expectations of its readers. *Chasing Mission Fit* is a must-read for anyone pursuing excellence in higher education marketing."

—**Marc Whitt,** higher education and nonprofit PR strategist, relationship builder and author of *PR Lessons Learned Along the Way and When In Doubt, Make Applesauce! Core Habits of the Masterful Public Relations Professional*

"*Chasing Mission Fit* stands as a beacon of hope for small colleges, especially small church-related colleges, grappling with the challenges of sustaining robust enrollments. Going beyond a mere guide, this invaluable resource serves as a strategic roadmap for college executives and enrollment leaders as they navigate the complexities of the higher education market. The book's potency lies in Bart Caylor's pragmatic 'how-to' approach, providing guiding recommendations and methodologies to construct effective marketing strategies aimed at reaching, enrolling, and retaining mission-fit students. Drawing on his extensive experience in college admissions and marketing, Caylor presents a straightforward market assessment model, social media strategies, and a plethora of recommendations tailored for colleges with limited resources. In essence, *Chasing Mission Fit* delivers on its promises. It is an essential read for anyone invested in the success of small, mission-driven colleges."

—Jeremy M. Lord, Retired President, J. M. Lord & Associates, Inc.

"*Chasing Mission Fit* takes the niche audience of higher education enrollment marketers on a clear theoretical and tactical path to success. Whether you're new to this industry or a veteran, you'll find the direction you need to take the next right steps. Rookies will find a complete roadmap; experts will find a stack of well-established strategies arranged neatly for execution. Caylor, with his unique background in tech, private sector business, and enrollment marketing, synthesizes advice from myriad higher ed experts into direct guidance to be immediately put into practice. He's the perfect person to lead this journey."

—Lindsay Nyquist, Associate Vice President for Marketing & Communications, University of Puget Sound

"This book should be essential reading for any higher education marketer. Bart has collected a wealth of insights from a variety of experts in their fields and added his own experience and knowledge. Higher education is facing numerous challenges, from the demographic cliff to the public perception of the value of higher education degrees. Adopting the audience-first strategy outlined in *Chasing Mission Fit* will help institutions succeed. Bart breaks down tactics and strategies that any higher education institution can employ to differentiate themselves in the landscape and to thrive in this challenging market. Covering everything from AI to print, this book dives deep into actionable steps you can start taking today to drive success for your institution."

—Brian Piper, Director of Content Strategy and Assessment, University of Rochester

"The Enrollment Cliff is no joke and it's right around the corner. If there is one book you need to read to help your team be prepared, it is Bart Caylor's *Chasing Mission Fit*. This book is written by one of the greatest legends in Higher Ed marketing and is critical for marketing and admissions teams to read as they prepare for the years ahead. This book won't just educate you about the coming wave and high level marketing strategies you should be exploring; it dives deeper into the practical steps you can take now to innovate and implement real tactics immediately, regardless of your budget, and to meet the new realities of Higher Ed that are upon us. Give yourself a gift this year and pick up a copy right now!"

—Adam Metcalf, Co-Founder and Chief Evangelist, ZeeMee

"Chasing Mission Fit by Bart E. Caylor is an essential read for higher education marketers, offering innovative strategies for student recruitment in today's competitive academic landscape. What distinguishes this work is its practicality, blending real-world case studies with actionable solutions. The book tackles some of the pressing issues of higher education marketing, including declining student enrollment and financial limitations, while providing key insights and considerations for higher ed marketers. The guide covers diverse topics, from cost-effective marketing to lead generation, presented in a clear, cohesive structure. If you've had the privilege to meet Bart Caylor, reading this book is like having a conversation with him. You walk away with valuable ideas and information that encourage and inspire you as you work to achieve your goals and increase marketing effectiveness. This book is a call to action for marketers in higher education, a valuable resource for both seasoned professionals and newcomers. It's a comprehensive toolkit, essential for enhancing marketing skills and effectiveness in the rapidly evolving world of higher education."

—**Dena Cambra,** Vice President for Marketing & Communications, Clarks Summit University

"Chasing Mission Fit by Bart Caylor is a game-changer in the world of higher education marketing. Here's why: In our crowded, attention-seeking world, standing out is crucial. Every brand, every institution is vying for a slice of our attention. This book understands that. It teaches that being different isn't just good - it's essential. But here's the twist. Caylor flips the script on constraints. Limited budgets? Small institution? He argues these aren't setbacks but opportunities to exercise creative muscle. This is a breath of fresh air in a world where big budgets

often dominate the conversation. The heart of the book is about finding the right fit. Not just *any* student, but the one who connects with your message, values, and mission. It's about quality over quantity. This isn't your run-of-the-mill marketing advice. It's a blueprint for thinking differently, for truly resonating with your audience. In essence, *Chasing Mission Fit* isn't just a book. It's a roadmap for small institutions to make a big impact; to find their voice in a noisy world. It's about making every word, every campaign count. For anyone in higher education marketing, this book is not just a read; it's a must-have."

—Ardis Kadiu, Founder & CEO, Element451

"Bart Caylor's *Chasing Mission Fit* is an essential read for marketing leaders in academia. It masterfully balances practicality with readability, offering a treasure trove of insights and strategies vital for institutions navigating today's competitive landscape. The focus on mission-fit as a differentiator is particularly resonant, providing a clear path for resource-constrained institutions to make impactful strides. Caylor's approachable style, interspersed with relatable examples, makes complex concepts accessible to all levels within an organization. His forward-thinking inclusion of AI tools and emphasis on human relationships as the cornerstone of marketing success make this book not just timely, but future-ready. An invaluable resource for anyone committed to advancing their institution's mission."

—Raffi DerSimonian, VP & Chief Strategy Officer, ERI

"As a friend and colleague of Bart Caylor, I've witnessed first-hand his profound understanding of higher education marketing, eloquently captured in *Chasing Mission Fit*. With over 35 years of experience, Bart expertly addresses the 'enrollment cliff' challenge, the necessity for distinctiveness in a competitive educational sphere, and the art of impactful marketing within budget constraints. His insights into brand awareness and lead generation, underpinned by a robust framework of three marketing pillars, are a testament to his deep industry acumen. This book is a must-read, offering a perfect blend of Bart's extensive knowledge and practical strategies, essential for anyone looking to navigate the complexities of student recruitment and higher ed marketing today."

—**Troy Singer,** Digital Marketing Specialist / Cohost of
The Higher Ed Marketer Podcast, Ring Digital

CHASING
MISSION
FIT

CHASING
MISSION
FIT

A Marketing Guide to Fill Your Institution
with Students Who Will Succeed

BART E. CAYLOR

THE
**Higher
Ed**
MARKETER

PRESS

Chasing Mission Fit: A Marketing Guide to Fill Your Institution with Students Who Will Succeed
Published by The Higher Ed Marketer Press
Indianapolis, Indiana, U.S.A.

CAYLOR, BART E., Author
CHASING MISSION FIT
BART E. CAYLOR

Library of Congress Control Number: 2023924070

ISBN: 979-8-9897639-0-0, 979-8-9897639-2-4 (paperback)
ISBN: 979-8-9897639-3-1 (hardcover)
ISBN: 979-8-9897639-1-7 (digital)

BUSINESS & ECONOMICS / Nonprofit Organizations & Charities / Marketing & Communications
EDUCATION / Administration / Higher
BUSINESS & ECONOMICS / Education

Ghostwriter: Danielle Harward, Alliance Ghostwriting
Line Editing: Talysa Sainz
Author Photo: Wesley Dean, Intermotion Media
Publishing Management: Susie Schaefer, Finish the Book Publishing
Book Design: Heidi Caperton
Set in Adobe Caslon Pro 11pt

QUANTITY PURCHASES: Schools, companies, professional groups, clubs, and other organizations may qualify for special terms when ordering quantities of this title. For information, email caylor@caylor-solutions.com.

This book is printed in the United States of America.

Dedicated to the memory of Tim Fuller, friend and mentor.
1957-2023

TABLE OF CONTENTS

INTRODUCTION

Why should a student pick your school?

I'll give you a hint. It's not because your institution has a "close-knit community" or a "9:1 student faculty ratio." These so-called "differentiators" aren't actually that different from 90% of small to mid-level institutions, barring large flagship institutions.

On our *Higher Ed Marketer* podcast, Guy Kawasaki—who originally helped Apple market the Macintosh computer and is now recognized as one of the top marketers in the world—joined us and discussed his thoughts on campus tours. He has four children and has been on close to sixty campus tours with them. He said, "Every single tour starts with, 'I am a student here. I am really happy here. The classes are small, the professors are available…' So my advice to you is that you got to think about how you're unique and valuable as a college . . .I would like every college admissions director to go on five tours of other colleges and you will see you are all saying the same thing."[1]

Guy's observations underscore the critical need for educational institutions to dig deeper and identify what truly sets them apart from the crowd. Students will pick your school because you resonated with them on a personal level. Which means the value of differentiation, at a base level, is in the needs of your audience and how you can best support them. Do this, and mission-fit students—students that truly resonate with your message and find the most success at your school—will come knocking at your doors.

Prospective students have so many choices; they likely don't even know all of the schools available to them. Which is why you should focus on marketing to their needs, instead of your functions. When you identify your key programs, and how you have helped past students thrive, you can position yourself for future students on the same journey and make it so they simply can't ignore you.

Easier said than done, right?

I know as a marketing professional, you likely grapple with restrictive budgets, understaffed teams, and the pervasive misunderstanding of marketing as a luxury, not a necessity. It's an uphill battle. These challenges only get worse when board members play armchair quarterback and change their strategies on the fly simply because their nephew (who does marketing in his garage) tried something that worked. You'll also be faced with challenges of emerging technologies, silos, a crowded landscape of similar institutions, and the common "just throw more money at it" marketing strategy.

With all these challenges, it's easy to fall into the trap of believing that a large budget and a bigger team are keys to effective marketing. But this is not the truth. In a crowded landscape of similar institutions, the real challenge lies in defining what makes you unique. Without this knowledge, your message becomes part of the collective noise, and you create friction.

Meaning you slow your mission-fit student down from identifying you as the key to their future.

We, as marketers, need to reduce the friction people feel when searching for our institution.

As a first-generation student myself, I am deeply connected to the power education can have to transform a person's life. I believe that for students to benefit from the power of your education, they first need to find you among a sea of options. This book is tailored to higher education marketing professionals with the goal of helping you identify your niche, effectively utilize evergreen audience-focused marketing strategies, and reduce friction, so you can stand out to mission-fit students.

With three decades of design and marketing experience, I've collaborated with globally renowned brands such as AT&T, Motorola, and GE. And, in 2011, Caylor Solutions was born out of my desire to fuse best practices from corporate, non-profit, and education sectors together to serve education clients exclusively. From K-12 schools to higher education, we have created unique, authentic narratives for each. Which in turn has led to higher enrollment and brand recognition for these institutions.

I believe that every institution has a unique story that deserves to be told. And through this book, I offer you key insights and strategies to tell your institution's story effectively so you can fill your institution with students who will succeed.

If you're a smaller institution struggling to get new students, you're not alone. Many schools spend big on marketing efforts that still don't get them the enrollment numbers they need. They hope that if they spend enough, they'll attract the right students. And with $2.2 billion being spent[2] in higher education advertising in 2019, there is a lot on the line for schools who leverage these cookie-dependent tools. What happens when the money runs out? Or when you spend more money, but you don't get more students enrolled? Or when gatekeepers such as Google and Meta change the rules of the game?

These strategies aren't sustainable. But there is some good news. As a smaller school, you have an advantage. You likely represent a niche—even if you don't know what it is yet—which better positions you to find your mission-fit student. The value is in your audience. You may not have all the resources of a larger school, but if you hone in on the right students with the right needs, and use the roadmap I provide, your enrollment can skyrocket! Let me show you how.

THE ENROLLMENT CLIFF IS REAL

The shadow of an impending "enrollment cliff" has been looming over higher education since the onset of the pandemic. The chatter among higher ed professionals has become a debate. Will the enrollment cliff even happen? Do we actually have to make adjustments for it?

So let me settle these questions and be clear: A considerable decline in new students is expected. It will happen. And it will severely impact many institutions, especially those that rely heavily on tuition revenue.

If you are not prepared for it, you will flounder.

Tim Fuller, founder of Fuller Higher Ed Solutions, shed light on some startling statistics. According to the 10th edition of the Western Interstate Commission for Higher Education's (WICHE) report, Knocking at the College Door, the majority of U.S. states could witness a significant enrollment dip by 2037.

In the worst cases, some states might see their enrollment numbers plunge by as much as 24%.[3]

This cliff is not just a future phenomenon; the decline has already started. As of 2021, 70 American institutions have shut their doors within a 5-year span.[4] Noticeably, almost half of those were faith-based institutions. Which means the pressure is on! Schools are racing to justify their value proposition to potential students even before we face the full brunt of the enrollment cliff. A joint study by the Associated Press and Stanford University added more grimness to the picture: over 200,000 students disappeared from the public school system during the peak of the pandemic.[5] Scary, right?

But don't be quick to pin this crisis solely on the pandemic's shoulders. Covid-19— despite its far-reaching consequences—is just a symptom, not the cause of the enrollment cliff. The signs of this impending crisis were present way back in pre-pandemic times.

In late 2019, CUPA-HR, the College and University Professional Association for Human Resources,[6] published a study on falling U.S. birth rates, a trend that traced back to the Great Recession of 2008. Economic uncertainties led to fewer births, and despite an eventual economic rebound, the birthrate never recovered.

Now the number of 18-year-olds in the U.S., which will peak at 9.4 million in 2025, is projected to tumble down to 8.05 million in 2029—a 15% decrease. This dip won't only affect higher education but our labor force as well! Plus, geographic and demographic shifts will further complicate the landscape. Cold, snow-prone states are expected to face significant enrollment declines, while regions like Texas show enrollment growth. Notably, Florida is projected to witness an 18% increase in its student population by 2037[7] . . . so that's a win! Much of the enrollment growth will come from demographics who have historically been outside of traditional undergrad recruitment, such as first-generation, minority students.

But the numbers don't lie. As uncomfortable as they are, we can't avoid them. Currently, the U.S. has around 6,000 higher education schools[8], and my estimate is that about 10% of these will close in the wake of the enrollment cliff. Don't let your school be one of them. This isn't just chatter—it's reality. And it's coming fast. It will take more than a meeting or two to prepare your school to face the cliff; however, if you identify your mission-fit students and *listen to them*, there is light at the end of the tunnel.

Before you take a sigh of relief and say, "we don't have traditional students, so we are safe," this will catch up with all schools. Soon the enrollment cliff will challenge all aspects of higher education recruitment. The reality of the enrollment cliff means you can no longer rely on outdated marketing strategies. Every school, believe it or not, can meet their enrollment goals. If, and only if, they focus on creating a centralized plan which attracts the right—mission-fit—students.

There are students out there who desire precisely what you offer. The young photographer who wants to turn photography into a serious career, or the mother who wants to go back to school and get her MFA in writing are all looking for an institution that services their specific needs. It's your job to get your school in their line of sight with a flag that says, "I'm here, and I am the best choice for your future success!" The schools who will weather the enrollment cliff are those who identify who their mission-fit students are and assertively position themselves to be noticed.

But, if you fail to articulate your value to those students, your school will likely be at risk when the enrollment cliff comes along. Outdated notions like "If we just get more students at the top of the funnel, we will be okay" are dangerous. A simple increase in numbers doesn't suffice if they aren't the *right* students.

FIND YOUR MISSION-FIT STUDENT

Identifying your mission-fit student is a pivotal step in creating an audience-focused marketing and enrollment strategy. They aren't just students who'll get a degree from your institution; they're the ones who'll embody its spirit, embrace its culture, and become its best ambassadors in their subsequent careers.

Before diving deep into the student profile, it's crucial to review your institution's broader mission. What qualities, values, and aspirations define your school at a high level? Once you have a clear understanding of this, you can then dig deeper into specific programs, majors, or departments to further refine what a mission-fit student would look like in those particular academic settings.

To create a profile of your mission-fit student, consider these key areas:

1. Reflect on alumni who've both thrived at your institution and gone on to make significant strides in their careers.

   - Which of your alumni frequently return for reunions, maintain active ties, or contribute as donors?
   - Are there any success stories or case studies that you already use in your marketing material?

- What common traits or backgrounds do these alumni share?

2. Look at your mission and values and ask yourself what students have most aligned with your institution.

   - Which students have best embodied the values espoused in your mission?
   - Are there student organizations, initiatives, or programs that particularly align with your mission?
   - Who are the active participants or leaders in these areas?

3. Examine your offerings, be it a niche course, a renowned professor, a community initiative, or a celebrated extracurricular program.

   - Which students were attracted to these unique offerings?
   - How did they maximize these opportunities during their time with you?
   - Have any students been pivotal in expanding or enhancing these programs?

4. Do some research on the paths that successful alumni take after graduation.

   - What kind of industries or roles do your most engaged alumni gravitate toward?
   - Are there specific companies or sectors that repeatedly hire your graduates?

- Do your alumni pursue further education? If so, in what fields and at which institutions?

5. Look at data and feedback—surveys, social media engagement, alumni testimonials.

- Which students actively participate or engage in online communities related to your institution?
- Are there testimonials where students or alumni explicitly mention aspects of your institution that resonated deeply with them?

By asking these questions and delving deep into the answers, you'll see patterns and traits that define your mission-fit student. Remember, understand this isn't about exclusivity, but about ensuring that both the student and the institution find a mutual and enriching fit. Once you know more about your mission-fit student, you can take a closer look at the generation they are likely from and how you can best reach them.

GENERATIONAL AWARENESS

As the high school graduate supply dwindles, non-traditional students—online learners, adult learners, and people who have been to a higher education school but have not completed their degrees—will be a critical demographic for your school. So, you need to make non-traditional messaging a cornerstone of your enrollment marketing strategy. From Gen Z to Boomers, your audience has wildly different messaging preferences.

Because your audience isn't solely the traditional under-graduate student anymore, you have to broaden your outreach horizon. Remember, the goal is not just to speak, but to be heard, understood, and valued by your audience. To do that, you need to be aware of how different generations receive your message.

GENERATION ALPHA (2010-2024)

This emerging group is growing up entirely in the 21st century, surrounded by advanced technology, global connectivity, and environmental consciousness. Unlike previous generations, they have a worldview shaped by digital immersion, cultural curiosity, and a blend of education and entertainment known as "edutainment." Remember this generation's impression of education was formed by the 2019 COVID pandemic where they experienced hybrid and online education, so they are likely easier to connect with online.

To engage them effectively requires depth. I spoke to Mark McCrindle, Founder and Principal at McCrindle Research, on my podcast to discuss what made Generation Alpha different.[9] He wrote a book titled "Generation Alpha: Understanding Our Children and Helping Them Thrive"[10] and gave me unique insight. Unlike Gen Z's 8-second filter,[11] Gen Alpha is willing to dive deep when content captures their interest. You can blend educational content with entertainment to keep them engaged because this is their preferred method of learning and interact-ing. And remember, generative artificial intelligence is a part of their daily lives, not just a novel tech. Use it to personalize their experiences and make interactions intuitive. While it's early to pinpoint exact platforms, keep an eye on evolving digital spaces where they spend their time. AI-driven platforms, interactive

VR spaces, or other immersive tech environments might be their go-to in the future.

GENERATION Z (1997-2012)

This group, often referred to as "digital natives," grew up with smartphones, social media, and instant messaging. Communication for them is fast and fluid. They value authenticity and diversity. They are quite pragmatic, having grown up during the economic recession, and they place a high value on experiences rather than material possessions.

To reach them effectively, you should be brief, visual, and compelling. They have an 8-second filter when viewing digital content, and they quickly decide whether something is worth their time or not within those 8 seconds. Use platforms like TikTok, Instagram, Snapchat, and YouTube to reach them. They use text messaging extensively, so don't expect a return call. Make sure you engage with them with authenticity and transparency because they prefer brands and institutions that interact with them on a personal level. With the novelty and "retro" feel of some communications, Generation Z are often open and excited about receiving communications like direct mail. In a recent TikTok trend, we can see they even enjoy the printed edition of the New York Times!

MILLENNIALS (1981-1996)

Often coined the "me" generation, Millennials are tech-savvy and value collaboration and innovation. They seek purposeful engagement and prioritize work-life balance, and they too are likely to value experiences over materialistic possessions.

Millennials tend to research online extensively before making decisions, so be prepared to meet their search with information. They are active on platforms like Facebook, Instagram, and X (formerly Twitter), which are great places to showcase your institution's values and social responsibility—especially because millennials care deeply about these issues and prefer to align with institutions that share in their personal passions.

GENERATION X (1965-1980)

They are referred to as the "sandwich" generation because they are likely juggling care for both their children and aging parents. They value work-life balance and are known for their skepticism and independence. Plus, they were the first generation to grow up with computers, making them a bridge between digital and analog generations.

Generation X tends to prefer email over other forms of communication. They appreciate straightforward, practical information that helps them make informed decisions. While they are comfortable online, they also appreciate traditional forms of communication. You can call or mail them, and they will likely receive both well.

BOOMERS (1946-1964)

Boomers are known for their strong work ethic, goal orientation, and resourcefulness. They value respect, loyalty, and face-to-face communication. They were late adopters of digital technology but have since become quite comfortable with it.

While many are online, they also appreciate and trust traditional forms of communication, such as direct mail and print media. Unlike younger generations, Boomers don't shy away from phone conversations. Plus, they appreciate heritage and tradition, so these are great values for you to put front and center on your outreach. They are more likely to engage with content that highlights the history and values of your institution.

GENERATIONAL AWARENESS UNLOCKS COMMUNICATION

Surviving the enrollment cliff won't simply come from "buckling down"; it will come from better connecting with your mission-fit students. The main change you need to make to connect deeper is to move from informational marketing to "useful marketing," a term coined by Jay Baer in his book *YoUtility: Why Smart Marketing Is About Help Not Hype*. In his book, he defined useful marketing as, "Providing answers to nearly every question a customer could conceivably ask—before they think to ask it."[12] And that means being proactive, adaptable, and ever-present in our communication strategy.

Once you know who your mission-fit students are, and what generations they are likely a part of, you can focus on meeting your mission-fit students where they naturally are.

REFINE YOUR WATERING HOLES

If you enjoy watching wildlife out in nature, you've probably learned that if you go to a water source, you have more chances to catch a glimpse of the animals you enjoy. Watering holes like a stream, or even an artificial water source like a bird bath, attract animals daily as they come to get what they already need.

Instead of going out looking for wildlife, the wise nature lover positions themselves in a place where the animals will come to them.

As humans, we're not so different from our wildlife counterparts. Every day, we also go to the same sources to get our information, inspiration, entertainment, and guidance. These are our watering holes. While animals depend on watering holes for life-sustaining water, we depend on watering holes for community and news.

In these spaces, people come together to connect, to belong, and to get the knowledge they need to make decisions for their future. Because they're coming already for something they need, you don't have to drive traffic to these places. So, like the avid nature watcher, the wise marketer positions themselves where the target audience is already going to be and publishes their content there. When you do this, your mission-fit student is less likely to be put off by your content and instead is often grateful they came by it.

A common pitfall, particularly among smaller institutions, is trying to be a one-size-fits-all solution that advertises to everybody. This will not work! Your enrollment efforts will flounder if you merely broadcast your brand's message on a billboard. Now more than ever, it's crucial for institutions to find their niche community and engage with them. You need to find the watering holes your mission-fit students naturally exist within.

While every target audience will have a different set of places, they go to daily to get their information, inspiration, entertainment, and guidance, there are two main categories of watering holes you need to identify: digital and physical spaces.

DIGITAL WATERING HOLES

Of course, the first places that come to mind here are the bigger social media platforms like Meta (formally Facebook), Instagram, and X (formally Twitter). You can find communities on these platforms that form around hashtags and groups. But there are other digital spaces you might not have considered if your target audience is young.

As the once self-proclaimed as "The Front Page of the Internet," Reddit boasts over 52 million active users. Reddit forms its content around communities with interests in almost anything (like the subreddit dedicated to orange cats). With 18- to 29-year-olds making up the user majority, the website is teeming with marketing potential for younger generations.

Higher education marketers need to realize that hundreds of schools already have active communities centered around their school, like this subreddit for the University of Illinois Urbana-Champaign, r/UIUC. If they align with your brand, these subreddit communities are potential watering holes where your audience is hanging out.

If you're trying to connect your brand with a younger audience, you need to check out Discord. Created as a voice chat and messaging alternative for gamers in 2015, the platform has since then expanded to be a hub for thousands of servers covering everything from finance to fashion. Because of its beginnings in the gaming community, Discord boasts a male-centric collective audience. As of early 2022, 65 percent of Discord's user base was male. With over 140 million active monthly users in 2021, there's a good chance your young prospective student is familiar with Discord.

And don't forget other gathering areas that may be outside the social networks such as gaming platforms and the niche platforms serving those users like Twitch or other online communities that can be found on every imaginable subject: Taylor Swift, homeschooling, or both (google it).

PHYSICAL WATERING HOLES

Physical watering holes are the brick-and-mortar spaces where your audience goes to get that face-to-face interaction they can only get in the analog world.

Here are some examples of physical watering holes:

- Barber shops
- Boutique specialty shops (think record stores catering to hard core audiophiles)
- Religious community centers and churches
- High school teams
- Clubs (ex. Boys & Girls Club)
- Community centers
- Locally owned businesses
- Food pantries
- Neighborhood nonprofits

Unlike digital spaces, it's hard to be in many physical watering holes all at once. It will cost more in terms of funds as well as personnel and time to canvas these places and get your marketing messages there. But having a marketing presence in physical watering holes like the ones above tend to make a greater impact on the target audience as the space is more intimate and focused on the individual members of the community you're reaching out to.

To be effective, you've got to publish your messaging in places where your audience is already going to get their information, inspiration, entertainment, or guidance.

GO BEYOND TRADITIONAL

Your mission-fit student might not even be the quintessential 17-year-old high school student, ready to plunge into the undergraduate world. These students might form a significant part of your audience right now, but we know the enrollment cliff is coming, which will directly affect their numbers. Luckily, they are far from the only group that institutions should be targeting.

You should also be targeting:

1. Non-traditional students
2. Dual enrollment students
3. Graduate students

According to Forbes, "More than 25% of freshmen do not return for their second year in college."[13] Which means one in four adults who attended higher education school do not possess a degree. These are potential students for you! They are an untapped group who represent a sizable demographic which could bolster your enrollment numbers. Especially for schools that can offer flexible, adult-friendly programs. These could be adults who got sidetracked by life's plot twists—like having babies or chasing a dream. And now they're scouting for a flexible way to finish their education. For them, the comfort and flexibility of online education presents an attractive pathway. For you, it's a goldmine of potential students.

However, marketing to an adult student means your competition may be more from life and overcoming doubts than the other institutions you may typically believe you compete with. They might not enroll in your school the first time they see your advertisement. Not because they are saying "no," but because they are saying "not now, but maybe soon." Life might not be right for them now, but if they know about your school, and how it can help someone like them gain more advantages in life, they will keep you in mind and make plans to attend your institution. And any money they bring your way in five years is worth the advertising you've spent on them.

Next, don't forget about dual enrollment students. These are high school students earning credit through AP tests and concurrent enrollment classes. When you sell credits at a discounted rate to these students, your institution becomes the logical next step for that student. Which in turn creates a pipeline for you to rely on.

Finally, we turn our attention to graduate students—those fresh from their undergraduate studies and those returning after a few years in the field. Both are prime targets for advanced degree programs like MBAs. Much like your non-traditional students, they will likely appreciate the ability to find schooling which fits into their busy schedules and helps them advance into the next stage of their career.

All three of these different types of students are key to keep in mind when refining your mission-fit student ideal. Once you understand which ones you want to heavily target, you can find their most likely watering hole to reach them.

INFLUENCERS, DEMOGRAPHICS, AND PSYCHOGRAPHICS

Another key thing to think about when targeting your mission-fit student is who and what will influence them.

When aiming to connect with your mission-fit students, it's crucial to consider the various layers of influence that shape their decisions. Understanding the demographics—like age, location, and socio-economic status—will help you target your message effectively. But demographics only scratch the surface.

Going a step further, you should look at psychographics—values, interests, and lifestyle. These can dramatically influence how and why a prospective student chooses an educational path. For example, a student passionate about environmental sustainability will be more attracted to a school with strong environmental programs and an eco-friendly campus.

In our digitally connected age, don't underestimate the power of social influencers. Students are increasingly looking to YouTube stars, bloggers, TikTok, or Instagram influencers for advice and reviews on what school to attend. These digital personalities can sometimes exert as much influence as parents or traditional counselors, so consider how your institution engages with or could be reviewed by these platforms.

Different generations are influenced differently. While Baby Boomers might rely heavily on word-of-mouth and traditional media, Generation Z students are more likely to be influenced by social media and online reviews. Therefore, a multi-generational approach in your strategy could be beneficial. This could mean hosting webinars or virtual campus tours to appeal to tech-savvy younger students, while also holding traditional open houses and informational sessions for parents and less tech-savvy individuals.

A multifaceted understanding of who your mission-fit students are and what influences them is essential. Who are they? How will they most likely hear about education? What communication channels do they use? And, most importantly, what will they likely need to know about educational opportunities available to them? Tailoring your outreach to resonate with these key influencers and communication channels will yield a more effective, efficient strategy in attracting students who are the right fit for your institution.

Your website serves as the first port of call for most prospective students and their families. Make sure it speaks to who you are and why you specifically are the best school for them. It's your digital ambassador, painting an intricate picture of your ethos, programs, campus life, and unique selling propositions. These will actively sell not only your prospective students, but their family as well!

Parents, and even more so, mothers, play a crucial role as advisors in a student's decision-making process. And occasionally they are the decision-makers when it comes to choosing an institution. You cannot discount them. Think about the influence your parents had on your own life. Even if they did not decide where you went to school or what you went to school to study, it is likely they still had a big influence on your decision.

Recognizing the weight of outside influences on your students and incorporating it into your overall strategy is vital.

EMBRACE DIFFERENT ETHNICITIES

Have you ever watched the Disney movie "McFarland, USA?"

It's a heartwarming movie that revolves around the power of understanding and embracing cultural differences. Set in a small agricultural town in California's Central Valley, the film tells the true story of a group of high school students from an economically disadvantaged Latino community who rise above their circumstances through their passion for cross-country running.

As the students navigate their way through various challenges and obstacles, they learn that their cultural background and heritage can be a source of strength and unity rather than a barrier. And through their shared love for running, the students foster a sense of belonging and pride within the community. "McFarland" showcases the power of cultural understanding and highlights how embracing diversity can lead to extraordinary goals. And because the coach (played by Kevin Costner) embraced this diversity, his life changed for the better.

Your marketing strategy should do the same for your mission-fit student. Inclusivity is key. And that inclusivity needs to expand to involve their families, especially in cultures where collective decision-making is the norm.

Look at Hispanic culture. Here, education is often a family affair. Mom, Dad, and even Grandma play influential roles in deciding which institution will pave the way for their child's future. Particularly when parents are non-native English speakers, this decision-making process becomes even more collaborative. This cultural nuance requires a shift in marketing strategies. If your mission-fit student is Hispanic, your brochures, websites, admission forms— and every other cog in your marketing machinery—should have an option for the language your audience might use.

And these adaptations are not confined to Hispanic populations. Depending on your geographical region and student demographics, this could be as varied as Japanese, Portuguese, or any number of languages. The rule of thumb is simple: speak your audience's language, metaphorically and literally. Sensitivity to cultural nuances is a necessity.

Your institution should acknowledge that students aren't a monolithic entity, but a mosaic of different experiences and backgrounds.

2

MONEY DOES NOT EQUAL BETTER MARKETING

In marketing, excuses come easily. But the "We don't have the budget we need" excuse is one I constantly hear. It makes me want to erect a sign reading, "No whining!"

Budget should not hold you back.

I know limitations exist in any situation. Budget constraints, personnel issues, perhaps even time crunches are all a reality. But these limitations should never stop you from excellent marketing. Sure, the grass might seem greener on the other side—maybe other institutions have more budget than you. But wishing you have their budget won't do anything for your school. Your mission is to nurture your own patch of land.

Acknowledge your current resources, understand your boundaries, and strategize accordingly. While your coffers might not be overflowing like those of tech billionaires, you're far from empty-handed. Financial resources can be found in various corners like bartering or grant acquisition. But let's chat about quality over quantity here. While the occasional volunteer can pitch in, remember you often get what you pay for. Instead, consider raising funds outside the typical budget. Maybe a nudge to the Board, a special pitch to a passionate donor, or even a savvy bank financing move can get you the funds you need. Think about how to leverage what you have in the most effective way possible.

Sometimes, the most valuable resource you can tap into is not cash, but wisdom and experience. For example, some institutions I work with have board members doubling as marketing directors. That's right, they are donating their time. These individuals, who are often retired yet successful business people, possess a wealth of experience and are willing to donate their time. They capably step into a marketing director's shoes and drive the strategy forward.

A common misconception is that bigger budgets inevitably lead to better marketing. However, in my experience, this is not always the case. In fact, some of the most creative solutions emerge out of constraints and boundaries. Constraints force us to be more innovative, to think beyond the norm, and to find unique solutions. They are not blockers! Treating them as such is doing you a disservice.

Back in 1998, my marketing firm worked with Cisco Press Publishing. I was hired to help them build a new eye-catching website. For the project, I managed a new designer fresh out of school, and he put together a great website design. But once the client reviewed it, they returned with multiple revision requests. The designer was quickly frustrated that they didn't like his work right away. He felt overwhelmed, saying there was no way to incorporate all the changes within the parameters set. I understood where he came from; when we put our blood and sweat into a design someone doesn't like, it's easy to throw your hands up. So I said, "These are not obstacles. They are your boundaries. The best design often happens when you don't have the freedom to do everything you want. Now is the time to be creative."

We create our best work when we have limits that push us toward innovative solutions. A constrained budget is a limitation that can absolutely spur creativity. Instead of lamenting on what you can't do, focus on creatively maximizing what you can do. There's an art in achieving goals with non-traditional methods.

When I started Caylor Solutions, I knew I had to find clients and felt I had to do so with cold calls. But here's the challenge: nobody answers the phone now. Cold calls go unanswered and voicemails unreturned. Even if you do get a response, nobody wants to give you 30 minutes so you can pitch yourself to them. What was I to do?

So, instead I went another, different, and free route. I started a podcast. And on this podcast, I invited potential clients to share their insights on subjects they are passionate about. Talk about a lightbulb moment! During my podcast interviews, I broke out of the traditional sales mold and leveraged my time and resources to have a personal, in-depth conversation with potential clients. I didn't need a colossal budget to reach them. No ad or commercial could do for me what a personal hour-long conversation would. And to this day, it's how I contact prospects to build relationships and trust.

The beauty of this approach is its authenticity. In a world bombarded with advertisements and unsolicited sales pitches, the podcast avenue offers a breath of fresh air. It's not just about selling—it's about connecting. By inviting potential clients to speak on subjects they're passionate about, it positions them as experts and gives them a platform to share. In return, I gain their trust and respect, simply by listening and valuing their perspective. This mutual appreciation lays the foundation for genuine relationships. It is relationship marketing at its finest, where connections built on trust and genuine interest often lead to lasting business partnerships.

How do you make the most of a small budget?

GUERRILLA MARKETING

With guerrilla marketing, you use creative, low-cost, high-impact marketing techniques. The term borrows from guerrilla warfare, characterized by hit-and-run tactics used by smaller, resourceful forces against larger, less mobile armies. But the essence of guerrilla marketing is the same—being swift, imaginative, and resourceful.

Instead of buying a billboard or expensive TV commercial spot, what if your institution honed into the watering holes of your mission-fit students? If you are a Christian institution, you might look to a Christian music festival to promote your institution. Now, you could buy a sponsor's table like everyone. Or, you can tap into the power of QR codes which, Mike Harmon CMO at spokenote said, " . . . are like catnip for Gen Z."[14] Place unbranded QR code stickers around the venue, leading scanners to a fun video or a digital Easter egg hunt. It's innovative and memorable, making you stand out among others pitching and hawking their wares at the concert. And best of all—it comes without the cost of purchasing a table!

Another great example is Red Bull. Their target is extreme sports enthusiasts. How do they market to them? They sponsor high-octane sporting events, capturing these moments in

breathtaking videos. One such stunt involved two parachut-
ists in squirrel suits jumping from one plane and flying into
another![15] Red Bull even holds the record for the highest freefall
jump from space, dropping a man from 60,000 feet in the sky.[16]
It's audacious, captivating, and it resonates with their target
audience. These high-impact moments, shared on platforms like
YouTube, generate far more interest and engagement than any
traditional banner ad would.

You don't need a big budget to make a big impact. Guerrilla
marketing helps you maximize your reach and resonate with
cost-effective tactics. And these marketing techniques are often
borrowed from industries outside of higher education.

A sparkling water brand called Liquid Death made quite
an impact in terms of marketing. The company's name and
branding by itself polarizes opinion—you either love it or you
hate it. But the ingenious part of their marketing is how they
leverage this polarization. Because they get so many hateful and
angry comments about their brand, they created a Spotify album
called "The Greatest Hates Volume 3" where the lyrics of each
song are actual comments from "trolls" who have criticized them
on the internet. The playlist features songs like "Worst name for
a water company" or "F*** whoever started this" immortalized
within catchy '80s tunes.[17]

But why, you might ask, would a company do this? Why
would they want to bring attention to the critics they get? The
answer is simple. They know their mission-fit audience. The
primary market for Liquid Death is Gen Z and Millennials,
who enjoy '80s music and relish in making light of negativity.
Liquid Death even released a limited-edition vinyl of the album
for the truly devoted fans. This campaign isn't just funny; it's
clever. It takes the negativity and transforms it into something

engaging and marketable. It also reinforces the brand's edgy, unconventional image, which resonates strongly with their target audience.

Even criticism can be a marketing opportunity if you approach it with the right attitude. Guerrilla marketing doesn't always follow the rule book; in fact, it often writes a new one. But the key to it is identifying the "watering holes" we discussed in Chapter 1 and bridge the gap between your institution and your audience's daily routines.

There is a common technique I encourage faith-based schools to use that works every time. I encourage the client to find churches where their prospective students are likely to be members. Then, contact the church to find out when the youth group leadership meeting takes place. Once they know the date and time of the meeting, they can print custom boxes, cups, and sleeves emblazoned with the school's logo, then go out and grab a local crowd pleaser treat like donuts or cookies and pop them into the custom boxes. Then, for the cherry on top, they can swing by a popular coffee shop (Starbucks or something local) and fill up a gallon container of coffee.

Now here's the magic...deliver this entire package to the leadership with a simple message, "Just wanted to bless you today, and share a bit about our school, {INSTITUTION NAME}. We hope to tell you more soon."

You can bet they will talk about your school during their leadership meeting. Finally, I encourage my clients to follow up a few days later and offer to take the youth pastors out for lunch. They are likely to accept the invitation with your previous package in mind, and you've just created an opportunity to chat about your institution to a key influencer and often gatekeeper.

It's a creative, non-traditional marketing tactic that makes a lasting impact with very little cost and effort. Try it out!

LOOK OUTSIDE EDUCATION FOR INSPIRATION

The most innovative solutions come from unexpected places. Look beyond the higher education sector for marketing inspiration. Often, it's more cost effective and can lead to the adoption of cutting-edge strategies that differentiate your institution.

STUDY COMPANIES

Businesses are spending thousands of dollars to figure out what works in their ad campaigns. Which means you can learn from their success and ask yourself how to apply it to your institution. Look to businesses that successfully target the same demographics as your mission-fit student. Companies like Apple, Target, Red Bull, Liquid Death, and Nike are targeting each generation very differently. Ask yourself—how do they utilize technology? What social media strategies do they employ? How do they personalize their messages?

For instance, in the late '90s, I did several marketing projects for Motorola. They were unveiling a groundbreaking concept: using cell phones for more than just voice calls. Tasked with leading the team, we set out to design online demos specifically for young audiences, showcasing these novel features. Most people hadn't even considered taking a photo or sending a text with their phone, so creating demos for features many were unaware of was both a challenge and an absolute thrill.

Simultaneously, I was also creating Anderson University's inaugural website in 1998, one of the first higher education websites I had put together. And the epiphany hit me: The investment and strategies Motorola was deploying to connect with younger users could be beautifully translated to the educational sector.

From there, it was easy to adopt those strategies for the institution.

Even now, I study the top ads a demographic loves before crafting my campaign for them. If a retail brand like Target is getting a lot of engagement on Instagram, I research strategies they are using and see how they can translate into how I want to attract an audience. You don't have to reinvent the wheel! While you may not have access to specific data, you can observe the marketing strategies companies are using and pay attention to the ones that gain traction.

This approach, of course, requires critical thinking and creativity. The marketing tactics that work for a technology company or a clothing retailer won't necessarily work verbatim for a higher education institution. However, by understanding the underlying principles and adapting them to the specifics of higher education, you can create compelling marketing strategies.

STUDY TRENDS

The digital age moves at lightning speed, and what worked yesterday may not work tomorrow. Social media platforms, for instance, are continuously evolving, with new features and algorithms that can significantly impact your marketing strategy. Similarly, consumer behavior and preferences shift rapidly, influenced by various factors from cultural shifts to global events.

A remarkable example of this is Taylor Swift. Her popularity stems from her strong connection with her fans. She responds to them, shows up at people's weddings, and sends videos to them. That one response lets everyone else know she might do the same for them. She even yelled at a security guard to protect a fan at a concert! A book shop owner next to a popular stadium during the Eras tour once said they dreaded the typical concerts at the stadium because the streets got so busy and littered with trash, and nobody came to their store. But Swifties were different. They came in, bought books, were kind, and cleaned up after themselves. It's a culture Taylor Swift has created. Her fans feel seen, heard, and valued, rather than just another cog in the wheel.

What can you do to make your students feel the same?

Another worthwhile approach is to look at historical methods and adapt them for today's context. A recent Kickstarter campaign had wild success and I couldn't believe what they sold. A 23-year-old developed a digital version of a disposable camera. This device, which only takes 28 photos and requires a 24-hour wait for photos to "develop" before they can be transferred via bluetooth to a phone, resonated with thousands. They raised $350,000 on Kickstarter![18]

I couldn't believe it! I grew up with the difficulty of a film camera where you had to wait to have your photos developed before you could see them. Yet, now that pain point is novel, it's celebrated and embraced, and it is what made this Kickstarter campaign so successful. In the context of higher education, this could translate to mixing traditional elements of the schooling experience—like personalized attention from professors or hands-on learning opportunities—with modern technology. Perhaps it means offering unique online learning experiences that balance the convenience of digital education with the personal touch of in-person classes.

By examining trends, you gain a deeper understanding of what captivates your target demographic. Trending hashtags and viral challenges aren't just fleeting moments; they reflect the cultural pulse, offering a goldmine of ideas for your campaigns. This approach allows you to skillfully weave your institution's core values with fresh, timely content, ensuring both relevance and authenticity. And it's yet another way you can create better marketing tactics without spending more money.

ASSESS BEFORE INVESTING MORE

Don't get caught in the trap of throwing good money at a bad marketing solution. While it's true that some strategies require a certain level of investment to be effective, simply throwing more money at a problem won't solve it if the approach itself is flawed. This principle applies as much to higher education marketing as it does to any other sector.

The Ford Edsel is a great example of money in the wrong strategy.[19] Ford rolled out the idea for a new car model in the late 1950s and planned for the car to be a mid-range option. One of its most memorable features is the "horse collar" grille, a vertical oval in the front that was quite different from the horizontal grilles commonly seen at the time. The car was also larger and beefier compared to many of its contemporaries, with pronounced tailfins and chrome accents, which were intended to convey a sense of luxury and sophistication.

Ford thought this car would be the one everyone wanted in the future, and they spent a lot of money making and advertising it.

But it turned out people didn't like how it looked, thought it was too expensive, and didn't see anything special about it compared to other cars. Despite all the money and effort Ford put into it, the Edsel was a flop.

Simply throwing money at a bad product won't make it successful.

Before deciding to spend more, stop and assess your strategy. Is it working as intended? Is it attracting the right audience, conveying the right message, and achieving your goals? If the answer is yes, then you might consider investing more to scale up the successful strategy. But if it's not hitting its targets, then pouring more money into it won't help. More at the top of the funnel isn't good if it's just more names and not mission-fit students.

You have to see the movement of the needle before you keep investing. Investments should be data-driven decisions. If there's clear evidence that a strategy is working—if you're seeing "movement of the needle"—then it might be worth committing more resources to it. However, without such evidence, increasing spending can often lead to a waste of resources. Adding more prospective students who aren't a good fit for your institution doesn't help anyone. It inflates your costs without increasing your results, leading to lower efficiency and effectiveness in your marketing efforts.

Before you decide to increase your marketing budget, make sure your current strategies are working well. Only then should you consider investing more. It's not about spending more, but about spending smart.

FIVE MONEY WASTING MISTAKES

There are several money-wasting mistakes I have seen clients make which you can avoid. Saving money is great. It's part of being a responsible steward of your marketing budget. But when doing so, you need to avoid short-term thinking that overlooks the potential long-term consequences. You need to make sure that the decisions you make today won't negatively impact your institution's ability to achieve its strategic goals in the future.

Here are a few mistakes I commonly see clients make which you can avoid:

MISTAKE #1:
HIRING THE PERCEIVED MARKET LEADER

This mistake often occurs when institutions assume that the best-known or most expensive marketing agencies will provide the best service for their needs. There will always be high-rate marketing agencies that serve as 800-pound gorillas who will charge you large amounts of money for their work. But there is a danger in following the crowd and going with these popular companies. You can do this work for less, and you shouldn't follow this crowd because it's not your crowd.

They might be the best ad agency in the region, but do they have higher ed experience? Likely no. You are selling something different. Your audience is not the "general public." Hiring the perceived market leader, just because they are the best in the region, doesn't mean they are the best for you. I recently had a conversation with a team who wanted to hire the marketing agency for the local successful tractor dealership, saying, "They are so good, everyone knows about the tractor dealership because of them!" Your school is not a tractor dealership, car wash, or credit union and doesn't have the same marketing needs. Marketing should be customized to the specific mission-fit student an institution wants to attract.

Larger agencies often bring a wealth of experience and can craft polished campaigns. However, the key for institutions is to find an agency that truly understands and resonates with their unique audience. Several schools have shown me their budget where they spent large amounts of money with the local newspaper, television station, or cable company for a pay-per-click (PPC) campaign. But using these resources may often get your school lumped in with the credit union, car dealership, and corner cafe in town trying to market their business to the general public with ads that are ineffective and often farmed out to overseas talent. Which means you aren't targeting your mission-fit student, and it makes local broadcast resources a less than ideal place to put your marketing dollars.

A more tailored approach is needed, which might come from either a niche agency or a larger one with specific expertise in your sector. It's not always about the size of the agency, but rather their fit and familiarity with institutions like yours. Always consider the track record and alignment of an agency's values and strategies with your institution's goals.

MISTAKE #2:
USING THE LOWEST COST OPTION

Opting for the lowest-cost option can lead to subpar results. Sometimes, you get what you pay for. Lower costs often mean less experience or expertise. Hiring an alumnus for a website redesign might save money upfront, but if they lack experience, it could lead to a website that's not optimized for your goals. Or, when working with a local digital marketing agency with no higher education experience, they might not understand the specific challenges and strategies needed for higher ed marketing. The key is to make smart decisions about what is essential and what you can do without.

MISTAKE #3:
TRYING TO SAVE BY NOT TAKING ACTION

In the effort to save money, many schools push off updating marketing materials like view books, travel pieces, printed materials, emails, messaging, social media, and even their website. This might save you a buck. But if your materials are ineffective and don't speak to prospective students, the long-term costs could be far greater than what you save. Those lost prospective students are a real cost. When you take them into account, your efforts to save money could actually cost you quite a bit.

MISTAKE #4:
TRYING TO DO IT ALL YOURSELF

Depending on the size of your marketing team, handling things in house might seem like an appealing and cost-saving solution. But, it's rare for a team to have the expertise and capacity to do everything in marketing well. Outsourcing certain tasks to specialists can ensure a high standard of work and free up your team to focus on what they do best. If your team is producing your own blog content but doesn't have a strong grasp of SEO and content strategy, then this channel will not be nearly as effective as it could otherwise be. It can also provide insight into other ideas, creative solutions, and options that may be hard to see by your team.

MISTAKE #5:
NOT INVESTING IN THE RIGHT TOOLS

There is no shortage of software tools designed to amplify and refine marketing strategies. But sometimes the tools we're most familiar with aren't necessarily the best ones for our current needs. I honed my skills on the Adobe platform throughout my career, but emerging tools like Canva present an innovative, more user-friendly alternative for faculty and staff, allowing them to use branded templates designed and overseen by the marketing team. This self-service model can lead to more cohesive branding and greater efficiency.

However, the trap that many in higher ed marketing fall into is sticking with familiar yet outdated tools, leading to over-investment. With tight schedules and even tighter budgets, it's challenging to keep pace with the newest tech. But that's the thing about staying current; sometimes, it means embracing new systems that offer better value for money.

MARKETING ON A
SHOESTRING BUDGET

For many higher education marketers, there's a familiar sense of unease: watching your budget dwindle as enrollment goals keep climbing. The good news? In today's digital marketing landscape, you don't need a budget on par with Coca-Cola to generate more leads for your enrollment department.

Institutions try to bolster their brand awareness via conventional means like billboards and television ads, banking on the premise that the more people they reach, the more students they'll attract. And while there is a time and place for brand awareness, it's not the silver bullet some think it is. I've heard many clients say things like "no one knows who we are" or "we are the best kept secret." But sometimes this is a good thing! It's okay if those who don't know about you aren't your mission-fit students.

Your audience isn't the entire city!

The number of people in a city population who genuinely want the type of education you offer—especially if you are a niche institution—is small. So splurging on widespread brand awareness campaigns is a misallocation of resources. You might look at larger institutions splurging on extensive TV and billboard campaigns and assume that's the only way to market. But it's not. While it's true that "you have to spend money to make money," your institution might not have to spend money the same way others do.

The narrower your target audience, the less money you need for general brand awareness. Instead, that budget can be used more effectively and creatively with a tailored approach. More than ever, marketing tools have become widely accessible, and the channels through which your audience wants to be reached have evolved significantly.

And the cornerstone of these changes is content.

Content is the fuel your marketing engine requires. Just like an older reliable car—your marketing might not look flashy, but with the right content, it can reach its destination just as effectively. Digitally-based content can be your secret weapon, driving the results you need to meet your marketing goals. Effective targeted content can reach your audience where they already spend their time, and when done well, it can engage, inform, and persuade in ways traditional advertising often can't.

Arguably, one of the most impactful marketing and communication campaigns in history involved a humble group of 12 men in the Middle East. Tasked with spreading the word of their faith, starting in their local town, to the region, and then to the ends of the earth, these early evangelists didn't have the benefit of billboards or newspapers. Instead, their primary means of communication was word-of-mouth, driven by the social proof people witnessed. And we see echoes of this in business today. Guy Kawasaki, calls himself a Chief Evangelist Officer, first for Apple Computer and now for Canva, because the term "evangelist" translates to "bringing the good news," and he proudly says that it perfectly describes his role.[20]

Your content should evangelize your institution and inform the right people.

Because when you inform and solve a need, you become relevant in the world of your mission-fit student. Look at how quickly ChatGPT has grown! Despite not having a significant marketing campaign, ChatGPT attracted a million users in just a week—an astonishing feat. Especially when compared to X (previously Twitter) which took about 2 years and Netflix which took about 3 years.[21]

Why did this happen? People respond quickly to opportunities that fulfill a need, and they talk about those opportunities eagerly. That's precisely why word-of-mouth marketing and targeting your specific "watering holes" can be so effective. These strategies foster authentic connections and deliver your message directly to those who are most likely to value and act on it. And guess how much money word-of-mouth marketing costs you? Zero!

Marketing on a budget is not for the faint of heart—it demands grit, determination, and a willingness to put in the time. Not every strategy you try will be a success. Which is why I encourage you to embrace the philosophy of failing forward. Don't worry about getting everything perfect on the first go, because it won't be. Try a new tactic, learn from it, and then refine your approach. This is 1000% better than doing nothing at all.

No one feels as if they have all the money they need to do their job right—so there's no use in dwelling on the "what ifs" and "if onlys." Your biggest competitive advantage is being different than all the rest. The following seven hacks will help you market on a shoestring budget while standing out against the competition.

HACK #1:
TAKE INVENTORY OF YOUR MARKETING AND MEDIA ASSETS

Joe Pulizzi, in his book *Epic Content Marketing*, advises marketers to view the content they create for their channels as valuable assets because they can repeatedly contribute to the company's growth.

No one does this better than the Walt Disney Company with their Classics Collection titles. Walt Disney stories like Snow White, Bambi, and Beauty and the Beast are content assets that generate sales revenue with minimal additional expenses year after year. In the same way, you need to build an inventory of evergreen content assets that you can use year after year in your marketing campaigns.

And here's the good news: Not all your content assets have to be created from scratch or require paying someone to do so.

Despite the fiscal crunch you may feel, chances are you've got resources you might not be fully utilizing. Do an inventory of all the physical and content assets your department already has, including:

- Recorded seminars and lectures
- Lighting and audio equipment

- Books, articles, and research your executive staff, board members, or faculty have created
- Original music and art from students
- Student testimonials
- Past blog posts, infographics, page copy, ebooks, etc.

Once you complete your inventory, you'll likely realize that you have more resources available than you initially thought. By repurposing this content for your marketing, you could potentially save thousands of dollars and make the most of the assets you already have.

HACK #2:
DEVELOP A ROBUST MARKETING STRATEGY

In some respects, tight budgets can be a blessing in disguise, compelling you to scrutinize your spending and get innovative with your planning.

When granted large budgets, many marketing teams can become careless, spending lavishly on "cool" campaigns that do little to meaningfully drive outcomes. But with a limited budget, you have to sit down and create a robust digital marketing plan using strategies that are most likely to give you the highest rate of return per dollar spent.

To be clear, robust doesn't mean complicated!

A "complicated" strategy might never see the light of day because there's just too much to do. A robust strategy, on the other hand, addresses all the fundamentals of good marketing:

1. Personas: Who are your target audience(s) and what are their needs? Spend time with your target audience to

understand their needs and perception of your institution.

2. Messaging: What values and offers should your marketing present to the audience?
3. Conceptualization: Make decisions about colors, typography, layout, and navigation design.
4. Wireframes: Move your concepts onto paper through hand sketches, vector graphics, or a keynote slide deck. It's important for everyone to see how the copy and design will look for your marketing materials before the content creation process begins.
5. Focus Groups: Validate and test your strategy to see how your target audience responds to what you've created.

By taking the time to nail down all the components of your marketing strategy, you will save money and stop trying to focus on marketing campaigns that never would have worked anyway.

Remember, at this point in the process, you haven't spent a penny!

HACK #3:
CREATE AN ENROLLMENT-FOCUSED WEBSITE

Higher education institutions have a plethora of departments, programs, and initiatives you could feature on your website. But for the greatest results, you should restrict your website's primary focus to enrollment needs.

When enrollment thrives, it's much like a rising tide that lifts all boats. For the lion's share of institutions, enrollment is the key cashflow department where much of the net revenue comes from. So if you increase enrollment, you can increase budgets across the board. And when enrollment is down, budgets are constrained across the board.

If your website centers on enrollment—rather than just showcasing your school's achievements—it removes friction and makes it clearer and easier for people to choose your school. And luckily for you, the entirety of Chapter Seven will be dedicated to this topic.

Once this website is set up, you should use all your marketing channels to drive traffic to your website. Content does you no good unless your target audience consumes the content. It needs to be built to encourage them to find your content and share it with their friends who have the same questions. So use your social media channels (free!) to constantly drive traffic to your website.

And don't forget to use your print materials like direct mail and brochures to drive traffic online. QR codes are fantastic for this. If you are already budgeting to create mailers or a magazine, these QR codes are a great way to use physical marketing materials to bring your prospective students to your digital world.

HACK #4:
CRAFT USER-FOCUSED CONTENT

Content is the number one way to market with a shoestring budget—hands down. Chapter 4 will go into detail on what content you should make. But a good stat to remember is, per dollar spent, content marketing generates 3 times the number of leads than paid search does. And content marketing drives higher conversion rates than traditional marketing by 600%![22]

But there is a catch. You have to produce content that your audience actually wants to consume. How do you do that?

Answer your audience's questions!

Content makes you and your organization the authority on whatever you choose to publish if that content consistently answers the questions people have. Every time a person goes online, they want to find the answer to a question. When they open their search engine, they literally type in the question they have in their mind, then Google finds the answer. Which is why answering your audience's questions around higher education is the key to increasing traffic to your website and other digital content. The best part is answering these questions doesn't cost much—if anything—to do, and the traffic it produces is organic, which is another word for free.

Anderson University, Indiana, (AU) sought my help because they were faced with a sudden decline in applications and enrollment after a decade of steady growth. They urgently needed to enhance their visibility and boost enrollment. When they partnered with Caylor Solutions, we found a heavy need to leverage SEO, social media, and other content marketing strategies.

The collaborative effort resulted in the launch of a new, enrollment-focused website and the implementation of a robust content marketing plan. With these changes, admissions traffic surged by nearly 25%! And search traffic saw an increase of almost 50%, with nearly half of that traffic being new visitors. Plus, they saw a year-over-year net change in enrollment increase by 15%. With the processes we put in place, their content marketing strategies also fostered a sense of community, with a remarkable 85% of social network members staying engaged and over 60% of students participating in new social networks. And the best part is these victories were accomplished on a shoestring budget.

HACK #5:
OUTSOURCE TO A DEPENDABLE PARTNER

Now, I know I operate a marketing agency, so this sounds like a quick pitch, but it isn't. The value of outsourcing certain aspects of your marketing strategy and content-creation work cannot be understated. It helps keep your operations lean and efficient, and it is a strategy that I have personally used consistently, which saves me a significant amount of money and time.

In the current freelance-driven, location-independent economy, finding the right person or agency for your needs has become easier and more cost-effective than ever before.

Outsourcing offers two main financial benefits. First, you can secure top-tier talent at a fraction of the cost. Second, rather than just one individual, you will gain access to an entire team for less than the cost of hiring a full-time marketing executive, which likely encompasses strategists, writers, designers, and more. If you haven't yet tapped into the advantages of outsourcing to supplement your marketing team, I strongly recommend considering it. Not only can it save you thousands of dollars in talent search costs, employee wages, and benefits, but it can also spare you countless headaches along the way.

HACK #6:
ARTIFICIAL INTELLIGENCE IS YOUR FRIEND

AI can assist in generating fresh ideas, streamline administrative tasks, and free up more time for creative endeavors.

Suppose I need ten unique ideas on a particular topic. I can simply ask ChatGPT, and within moments, it provides suggestions, saving me valuable research and brainstorming time. Or if I require a quote from a specific author on a specific subject, I can ask Perplexity.ai to find it, and it will reference the source, saving me the time I'd otherwise spend combing through numerous texts.

Robots are not going to take your job. But the people who know how to engage robots will. As you learn how to use these tools, you won't lose opportunities, but you'll get more opportunities because you know how to do a task faster and more cost effectively than others. Which is why integrating generative AI into your work is essential.

DEWALT Tools uses robots, or "co-bots" as they prefer to call them, to collaborate with their human workforce in the manufacturing process. They understand the importance of using robotics and AI to enhance human effort. Personally, I save about 10-15 hours a week using ChatGPT, whether it's for generating outlines, brainstorming ideas, or other tasks.

One warning though. Currently, generative AI is the wild west. You can get lost in the ethics of it. To me, generative AI isn't plagiarism because I could have given my assistant a "feeling" of what I want, for content, and they will research what's been done and come back with it. Don't let yourself get caught in the "should I" or "shouldn't I" of the tool. Instead, utilize it now and adapt as its legal landscape changes.

HACK #7:
RECYCLE BUSINESS IDEAS

Recycling business ideas, or drawing inspiration from existing concepts, is a powerful strategy in the world of marketing. It's worth observing what businesses are doing outside of your industry and considering if their tools or strategies could be beneficial in your context. Don't limit yourself to only tools that were specifically created for higher education. Take, for instance, Canva, a consumer product. Even though it wasn't designed with higher education in mind, it can still be a valuable tool in this field, and because so many institutions have started using it, they now market directly to higher education.[23]

The goal is to be aware of cultural trends and developments in other industries. Then brainstorm ways you can adopt those ideas for your purpose. It's also valuable to keep a finger on the pulse of what your prospective audiences are interested in. What are your kids watching or consuming? Where are they spending their time? Concentrate on their world and figure out how to repurpose it for higher education.

For instance, Oscar Mayer's strategy with their Wienermobile,[24] is a great idea to copy. They visit grocery stores, provide food to patrons, and distribute coupons for their products in the store. This mobile and gigantic hot dog draws the eye and directly markets their products. Why not steal the idea? If you are marketing a nursing program, you could wrap a food truck with your school's name and logo and travel to different hospitals, offer lunch, and have an admissions team on-site distributing brochures. This allows direct engagement with your target audience without the presence of competitors.

I hope these hacks help you create high-quality, targeted marketing on a shoestring budget. Marketing on a shoestring budget is not just about scrimping and saving—it's about smart decision-making, strategic resource allocation, and adaptability. But I do feel there is one more thing to note.

A BIG TEAM DOES NOT EQUAL BETTER MARKETING

Contrary to what many might think, having a bigger team does not necessarily equate to better marketing. Especially when you operate on a shoestring budget.

In traditional higher ed marketing, there's a tendency to assemble a team that covers every possible role—a designer, webmaster, copywriter, creative director, marketing strategist, and so forth. It's like trying to fill every seat on a bus based on distinct skill sets. However, this approach may not always be the most practical or effective, particularly when resources are limited. You do not need to fill every seat with a different specialized skill. The key lies in strategically filling your team with versatility and adaptability rather than specialized skills.

Instead of having an assortment of specialized "surgeons," consider employing a team of "family practice doctors." These are individuals who possess a broad understanding of various marketing aspects and who can effectively diagnose what is needed. They may not be the best at executing a highly specialized task, but they know when a specialist is needed and how to find one. Diagnosing and problem-solving are highly valued qualities that trump the ability to execute in isolation.

I recently advised a school that wanted to hire both a photographer and a videographer. I suggested they combine the two roles and invest the saved salary into specific project needs they could outsource to freelancers on platforms like Fiverr. This worked wonders for them! Especially when they needed to create content. Instead of hiring a full-time expert, they contracted a part-time individual from their target audience who created more engaging and authentic social media content than they could have done on their own!

SMALL TEAMS ARE AGILE

On the surface, a large team may seem like a good idea, especially given the extensive work that marketing demands. However, the reality is that bigger teams often require more resources, both financially and in terms of management, and can lose the ability to adapt quickly to change. But small teams embody agility (the ability to rapidly respond to changes as they occur) and can pivot as needed.

Alvin Toffler in his book *Future Shock* said, "The illiterate of the 21st century will not be those who cannot read and write, but those who cannot learn, unlearn, and relearn."[25] I wholeheartedly agree. Being adaptable—or open to change—is good, but not good enough. We also need to be highly agile in our approach so we can pivot as the world pivots around us. You can't afford to wait years to implement changes; we have to implement changes quickly. And typically, small agile teams do this really well.

An oversized team might seem like a good idea on the surface—especially with the amount of work marketing has—but the truth is that the larger the team, the more entrenched and specialized it becomes. You need more money to keep them. More processes to manage them. And you can bet flexibility goes right out the window.

But, a small, nimble team can be flexible in their approach to projects and problems. They can handle more, adapt faster, and achieve higher goals. Just like in the account of David and Goliath.[26] David, who was small and nimble, armed only with a slingshot and five river stones, defeated the armored and slow-moving Goliath because he had the advantage of agility. David refused the armor offered to him by Saul both for the flexibility he needed in battle and his faith in God. Without the armor, he could move quickly and adapt to a need in the moment.

Your small team has the power to be both agile and adaptable so you can understand and integrate new concepts quickly. It's a hidden strength only small marketing teams get to experience. *Use this.* Just like David found, it is your advantage!

HIRING STRATEGIES I UTILIZE

Assembling a marketing team that is small, nimble, and powerful isn't just about ticking boxes on a list of qualifications—it's about ensuring a harmonious cultural fit and the ability to learn and adapt. Here's some insight into my hiring philosophy:

1. **Attitude and Cultural Fit Are Paramount:** When I'm considering a candidate, their attitude and character fit are the first things I look at. Skills can be taught, but attitude fit isn't something that comes with training. If a candidate doesn't mesh with your team or institution's values, it's best to move on, irrespective of their skills or abilities.

2. **Understand Your Institution:** Hiring for a faith-based institution versus an engineering school requires different cultural considerations. It's crucial that your new hires understand your institution and its unique attributes.

3. **Learning Ability Is King:** In a constantly changing landscape like marketing, the ability to learn and adapt is crucial. Even if a candidate doesn't have a deep understanding of your field, their curiosity and eagerness to learn can make up for it.

4. **Industry Experience Matters:** Just like you need a marketing agency with higher ed experience, you need team members who understand the nuances of your industry. What works in other sectors may not apply to higher education. Either hire someone who does, or provide them the necessary training (see #3 and #5) for success.

5. **Be Open to Training:** If a candidate has the cultural fit and learning ability, but lacks some experience, don't rule them out. There is flexibility here. Sometimes a unique perspective can be advantageous. Be open to investing time in training—they could turn out to be your most valuable player.

When hiring, don't just fill vacant seats. Each role should solve a specific problem or need within your team. If a role isn't contributing to your goals, consider whether it's truly necessary or if there's a more effective solution, like outsourcing. The goal is not to create the largest team, but the most efficient one.

4

BRAND AWARENESS VS LEAD GENERATION

Some higher education marketers have a misguided belief that the key to attracting more students is witty billboards and high-priced commercial slots. And while these things do create brand awareness—to the general population and not necessarily to your mission-fit student—true lead generation means speaking to the right person in the right place.

Billboards can be effective, especially for brands with widespread appeal. Think of them like the car wash ads: they target everyone because everyone could potentially need a car wash. For higher education, though, the audience is often more specific. While some larger schools have the reach and resources to make broad-scale advertising work, many institutions thrive by zeroing in on a particular niche. If we think about it, maybe only around 25% of your city's population might be looking into higher education. And within that subset, a smaller group will be interested in what your school specifically offers. The narrower your niche, the less effective broad-scale marketing becomes.

When institutions focus more on broad-scale brand awareness instead of lead generation, they may overlook the crucial difference between the two: the specificity and immediacy of the target audience's needs. Brand awareness is about getting your name out there and creating a level of familiarity and general reputation among a wide audience. The hope is that when the time comes for someone to make a decision related to what your brand offers, they will recall your name favorably and consider you in their decision-making process.

Lead generation is about directly targeting people who are actively interested or likely to be interested in what you offer and converting them into prospects or clients. This involves understanding who your target audience is and what they need and reaching out to them with a solution at the right time.

Which brings us back to the importance of watering holes!

The problem with focusing too much on brand awareness in higher education marketing is that it's less targeted and less timely. Brand awareness efforts might reach people who don't need a higher education degree or who aren't ready to make that decision. But lead generation finds and reaches people who are already interested in or at the stage of deciding to pursue a higher education degree. All you need to do is capture their interest and present a compelling case as to why they should choose you.

LEAD WITH DIFFERENTIATION

When you focus on lead generation instead of brand awareness, you should lead with what makes your institution different. Many schools look up to established, world-renowned institutions like Harvard and think, "If we were Harvard, we wouldn't need to market like this." And it's easy to fall into this trap, but it couldn't be further from the truth.

On my podcast, I spoke with Harvard's marketing team, and what they told me was illuminating. Despite being a prestigious institution with a centuries-old legacy, Brian Kenny, Chief Marketing and Communications Officer for Harvard Business School, said, "We have our own marketing challenges."[27] It takes constant effort to maintain their position, meet high expectations, and attract a diverse pool of high-performing students. It doesn't just happen simply because they are *Harvard*. In fact, I'd argue they embody the Harvard name and can be easily identified by it *because* of the efforts within their marketing department.

Every institution, no matter how established, faces its unique challenges. Harvard's brand power does not exempt it from strategizing and innovating in its marketing efforts. Their team continually refines their approach to connect with potential students across various demographics and geographic locations. And they do not try to be anyone else. They are simply themselves and have gotten extremely good at identifying their mission-fit students.

Each institution has its own strengths, culture, and value proposition. Rather than emulating Harvard or any other institution, schools need to focus on their individual attributes and nurture their unique identity. You should distill who you are as a school, and your marketing should lead with that differentiation. Do not lead with being a "small school" who has a "caring community" and "great academics." If I had a nickel every time someone told me that when I asked how they differentiate their institution, I could retire.

This simply isn't enough.

You need to dig deeper, seeking unique attributes that stand out. Schools may have specific features, like a focus on outdoor adventure or an unconventional grading system, which truly set them apart. A great tip is to ask your alumni you have identified as past mission-fit students why they chose your institution. Their answers might surprise you.

When trying to find your differentiators, the four Ps of marketing can be helpful. These are: Product, Price, Promotion, and Place.

Product refers to the programs and experiences offered. Price is largely outside the marketing department's control, but marketers should still have input on how to present it. Promotion includes both digital marketing and broader brand awareness efforts. And place refers to where promotional messages are distributed.

When trying to identify your unique features, consider these four Ps and assess where adjustments can be made. By leveraging these factors, you can enhance your relevance and ensure you're not missing valuable opportunities. Sometimes, even the Product, despite being slow to change, may need to be modified to keep up with market needs and demands.

"EVERYONE" IS NOT YOUR TARGET

Don't try to sell to everyone. I know of one very well-known institution that purchased nearly 100,000 potential student names. They marketed to these students, but did not get one enrolled from that list. Why? They likely either didn't clearly communicate a message that would resonate with their mission-fit student, or the list contained the wrong students, so the messaging was incongruent to the audience.

This isn't just a waste of marketing resources; it can lead to real-life complications for both the institution and the students. For example, a student could apply to a school under the impression that on-campus housing is available, only to discover later that it isn't. The result? A dissatisfied student and a waste of administrative resources that went into processing their application.

Given a choice, I'd opt for 500 applications from mission-fit students over 5,000 applications from students who don't align with the institution's values or offerings. If you are inundated with processing thousands of ill-fitting applications, you might inadvertently sideline the mission-fit students—the ones who should be your focus. And, when you ensure that your student body consists mostly of mission-fit students, you create a harmonious campus environment where students can thrive. Their satisfaction and success, in turn, positively reflect on your institution, enhancing its reputation and appeal to future mission-fit applicants.

Which is why I want to address that there is no silver bullet that will draw *everyone* to your campus. But you can define your mission-fit student and make a silver bullet for *them*. If you learn how to speak well to one type of student, and fill their need, your enrollment will only go up!

I do have one warning for you. Don't fall into the trap of equating your mission-fit student with academic prowess or financial capability. The ideal student shouldn't be defined by their GPA or their ability to pay tuition. Instead, this mission-fit student should align with the values and programs that your institution offers. You cannot speak to everyone. At least, not successfully. Not if you want to move away from the generalized marketing approach which many institutions are stuck using today.

If you are a rural faith-based institution spending marketing dollars in urban New York City, that may not be the best use of your money. Even if someone on your board is convinced a billboard in Times Square will get rid of your enrollment problems, it won't.

While multi-million-dollar campaigns on billboards and TV might seem like the perfect strategy, they often blur the line between brand awareness and lead generation. Hospitals can afford to engage in brand awareness campaigns with billboards because everyone, at some point, will need a hospital. Higher education, however, deals with a small portion of the population. The vast majority of people are not your prospective students, especially if your institution has a niche focus.

A targeted, mission-focused recruitment strategy contributes to a more cohesive, satisfied student body and a more efficient administrative process. Which means you can better service your target students as an institution.

PROGRAMMATIC MARKETING

Many students have a sense of their intended field of study, and they search for institutions accordingly. They're not just looking for any school—they're looking for the "best schools for X." By gearing your marketing strategy toward specific programs, your institution becomes far more discoverable in these searches. This is where programmatic marketing comes into play.

Programmatic marketing means selling the programs within the context of the school, and it is often an overlooked strategy. Instead they usually resemble course catalogs, organized by department, which can make it challenging for prospective students to find the information they are seeking. On a catalog-based website, a student interested in studying criminal justice might land on the website and be faced with a labyrinth of clicking before they find their area of study. They don't know that to find information about the criminal justice offering they have to click on "College of Social Sciences" then click on "Sociology Department" then they *might* find Criminal Justice if they don't have to click down further.

The average high school student doesn't know what courses and degrees are rolled up under specific departments. Nor do they care. Which is why the catalog approach does nothing to help your institution stand out.

However, if that same student searched for "best schools for criminal justice" and your school popped up because you have been marketing to that need, then the potential student knows exactly what you offer and why you are the best school for them. One of the best things you can do in your marketing is show students how 5-7 key programs can connect to the career outcomes they're dreaming of. That's how you attract mission-fit students who are genuinely interested in what your institution offers. You should aim to answer very specific questions like "I want to be an FBI agent. How do I do that and where do I go to learn?"

When crafting messaging around these programs, remember to write as if you are speaking to a first-generation student who has no background knowledge on how an institution like yours works. Many people landing on your site don't know the same information as your staff or those who come from families with a history of higher education. Your messaging needs to be simple, clear, and easy to understand.

Lastly, as a part of programmatic marketing, be clear to the prospective student on how much this program will cost them. Listing tuition on your site as "$375 per credit hour" with no further context is like visiting a furniture store and finding a table priced "per square foot." That's not what we want to know. If you try to make potential students do the math themselves, you are creating friction for them. Which makes it harder for them to pick your institution. Instead, give them an estimated final cost so they can budget. Something like "if you're pursuing ABC degree, it will cost about XYZ" is extremely helpful to new visitors on your site. Even a price range is better than offering credit per hour pricing.

The best thing you can do is keep things simple when presenting majors, outcomes, and costs. Students want to know: Will I fit in here? Does this school offer the major I want? Can I afford it? If your website answers these questions directly and succinctly, prospective students are more likely to come back to dig deeper and learn more. A focus on programmatic marketing helps outline these three points and also convinces the prospective student that your specific institution is an authority with a specific program.

SELL BENEFITS, NOT FEATURES

Many schools make the mistake of emphasizing features—whether that's the number of books in the library, the number of students on campus, or the variety of majors available. However, these details alone don't paint the whole picture and aren't necessarily interesting to prospective students. What they want to know is if you have the specific resources they need and if the environment aligns with their lifestyle and goals. Relying on features to promote your school is a risky strategy as there will always be bigger institutions boasting higher numbers. If you're selling based on features, there will always be another school out there that's "bigger, brighter, and smarter."

You won't win that game.

Instead, focus on benefits. Ask yourself, what makes attending your institution beneficial to your mission-fit students? What are the benefits of your school, and how do they help your audience? If sustainability is important to your target demographic, like many Gen Z students, highlight how your institution emphasizes sustainability in its campus operations and curriculum. Benefits are about painting a picture of the student experience and how it specifically aids your audience. This is what prospective students want when considering which school to attend.

The specific key here is *your* audience. If you are all things to all people, you are nothing to everybody. The quest to appeal to as many people as possible is a losing battle. And it often results in bland, nondescript branding that fails to stand out from the crowd.

One of the biggest obstacles to differentiating an institution comes from internal resistance. Faculty members may push back against highlighting certain programs or aspects of the school for fear of overshadowing others. But remember, your primary goal isn't to keep every department satisfied; it's to attract your mission-fit students. If nursing is a major program at your school, and it attracts hundreds of students each year, wouldn't it be beneficial to feature it prominently in your marketing materials? Balancing internal politics can be tricky, but if prioritizing the nursing program over the history major leads to more mission-fit students, it's the right move to make. After all, it's about the students you serve, not keeping faculty content.

The fastest-growing schools right now are those that take a stand and aren't afraid to define who they are. Some people might not like it, but those are likely not the people you want to attract. Rose-Hulman Institute for Technology, a highly ranked STEM-oriented institution in Terre Haute, Indiana, has been strategically leveraging social media to communicate its value proposition and attract students from diverse backgrounds. With a student population of around 2,200, the institution draws learners from all over the world.

Despite being a highly ranked and selective institution, Rose-Hulman still has to work diligently to meet its enrollment goals each year. They are well-known for their effective social media marketing. On Instagram and other platforms, they strive to surprise their audience with unexpected content, aiming to overturn common misconceptions about STEM fields. For example, they try to counter the belief that STEM lacks creativity or that its students are antisocial. By showcasing STEM's creative side and the collaborative, vibrant environment on their campus, they change these perceptions and attract their mission-fit students.

A key part of their social media strategy is the use of video content. Rose-Hulman uses a mix of short and long-form videos, including student-produced content, to demonstrate the practical application of lab work and the research students are conducting. These efforts, often coupled with an educational component, offer a clear picture of what it's like to study at Rose-Hulman.

But they don't stop there. To keep up with current social media trends, the school has started creating more vertical and shorter videos, with many of them acting as trailers for longer pieces. They are also active on platforms like TikTok, with student-produced content focused on raising more awareness for STEM fields.

Impressive, right? They have leaned heavily into what makes them different, and it informs their marketing strategy.

You can do this too. The goal is to make sure your potential students can self-identify as a fit from the beginning. You'd rather have people visit your website, understand what you offer, and quickly conclude whether you are a fit for them or not. This saves everyone's time—the prospective students and your admissions office—and ensures that those who apply are genuinely interested in what your school has to offer. Success lies in an institution's ability to differentiate itself in a crowded marketplace, and its benefits, not features, which will help you do so.

5

DON'T BE A SHORT ORDER COOK

"Make it look good and have it ready by Monday" is an all too familiar directive many marketing professionals have heard. And it's often referring to whatever bookmark, brochure, or banner internal teams feel they need.

But in truth, these quick service needs aren't the best way for higher ed marketing departments to spend their time. My podcast guest, Ethan Braden, who was the Executive Vice President, and Chief of Marketing and Communications at Purdue University and Purdue Global at the time, likened this to being a "short order cook," serving up fast, made-to-order designs rather than strategically driving the institution's marketing efforts.

Have you ever seen a short order cook at work? In a packed restaurant, they are in the kitchen, a whirlwind of constant motion. They're grilling burgers on one side, scrambling eggs on the other, and toasting bread, all the while keeping an eye on the fries in the deep fryer. Their world is the epitome of multitasking under pressure, and their success is measured in how quickly and accurately they can complete orders.

This scenario is chaotic and hard for many to keep up with. High demand and short timelines mean these cooks need to prepare meals quickly, often in less than fifteen minutes. And customers frequently customize their orders, so the cooks must be flexible and responsive, further adding to the chaos. These cooks also have limited resources. Whether it's the number of burners on the stove, the amount of prep space, or the availability of ingredients, short order cooks often have to work within tight constraints. To top it all off, they are constantly interrupted with new orders, disrupting whatever rhythm they might have established.

In this environment, planning can be difficult. Cooks are typically responding to what's happening in the moment—what orders are up, what needs more cooking, and what's ready to serve—rather than thinking about what they'll be doing ten minutes from now.

Now, translate this scenario to the marketing department who is flooded with banner requests and brochure needs. It's easy to see why they may struggle with strategic planning when they are constantly bombarded with quick requests from the faculty. These requests alone often eat up over 50% of their time from some leaders that I have talked to! Which means they are always reacting instead of proactively setting a strategic course. It's like trying to cook a gourmet meal in the middle of the lunch rush at a diner; the environment isn't conducive to thoughtful, strategic preparation.

This is why stepping away from the "short order cook" model and moving towards a "master chef" approach—where there is time for planning, preparation, and strategic thinking—is so beneficial for marketing departments. Ad-hoc requests cannot be the norm if marketing is to truly influence the school's bottom line. As Ethan told me, they have to move from being "driven" to being the "drivers."

Because marketers *should* be drivers. They should lead strategic initiatives to make a difference in enrollment using their marketing skills and insights. This doesn't mean disregarding input from leadership, but it does mean grounding decisions and strategies in professional marketing knowledge rather than the subjective opinions of non-experts.

Many marketers originate from creative backgrounds and often attempt to pitch ideas based on their creativity. While creativity is a crucial component of marketing, it's equally important to base decisions on proven best practices and data-driven strategies. And you cannot rely on creativity alone to get you there. Stepping into the role of a 'chef' means leading with expertise, influencing strategy, and driving success.

It's time for a change. It's time for marketing departments to have the authority to say "no," backed by the full support of the school's President. Not everyone will be happy. But learning new methods (like setting up self-service brand templates in a tool such as Canva or outsourcing to freelancers) could be the answer to these ad-hoc requests from campus departments, freeing the marketing department to focus on revenue-enhancing marketing.

DON'T KEEP DOING WHAT ISN'T WORKING

Time is an essential factor in higher education marketing. Unlike regular commodities that can be purchased anytime, higher education admissions operate on a cyclical timeline. Which means the process of finding what works and what doesn't needs to be done quickly through testing.

To truly understand what works and what doesn't, you need to give your marketing strategies enough exposure across different demographics and times of the year. Then you need to verify how potent they are. Tools like A/B testing can help evaluate the performance of different approaches. For instance, sending out an email with two different subject lines to see which one yields a better response rate.

You need to build a testing mechanism into your plan. It's crucial because it allows you to validate your strategies and ensure their effectiveness. And if you don't know what the best strategies are for the tactics you are using, you can use resources like ChatGPT for best practices or do comprehensive research on the strategies you want to adopt. With testing strategies in place, you can get the instant feedback you need on your marketing strategies.

When you get these results, listen to them. Don't keep doing what you're doing and just hope the results will improve. They won't. Persistence can be a valuable trait, but it's crucial not to mistake stubbornness for determination in your marketing strategy. One of the most common pitfalls in the marketing world is repeating failed strategies and hoping for different results. It is often said that the definition of insanity is "doing the same thing over and over again and expecting different results."[28] So don't be insane!

While it's human nature to hold out hope for a strategy to eventually succeed, the reality is that if something isn't working, simply continuing with it won't likely change the outcome. When you're busy, it can be easy to keep your head down and ignore this reality. However, such an approach often leads to problems worsening over time. It's far more productive to address an issue when it's minor than when it's spiraled out of control. By asking the right questions, you can better understand why your strategy is falling short and start making necessary adjustments. Rather than throwing everything out, constructive adjustments could transform a failing approach into a successful one.

When Things Go Wrong

First of all . . . don't panic!

The fastest way to make even bigger mistakes is to panic. Stay calm and decide how to manage the situation. Things only get worse when we get upset, panic, or become angry. Even our doctors are trained in medical school to keep calm in scary situations because they know an angry or panicked doctor is the quickest way to cause more harm than good.

No plan will flow perfectly without any hiccups. It's okay if your strategy runs into a few. That just means it's time to make a few adjustments. Having a plan that is not working isn't the end of the world. It's an opportunity to reassess and readjust. If you need to make adjustments to your plan, start by backtracking and pinpointing what's missing. Once you do that, you'll often gain clarity into the issues at hand and how they occurred. This is especially true if you didn't take into consideration the industry norms. Every industry and audience have unique characteristics that influence open rates, response rates, and other metrics.

For example, in higher education marketing, you may not achieve the same open rates you were used to if you came from another industry. Similarly, audience demographics significantly influence the type of responses you get. A Gen Z student might be enticed by a free sweatshirt, whereas an adult learner might appreciate a comparison chart of different schools. A one-size-fits-all marketing campaign isn't going to yield impressive results, and it's unfair for leadership to expect it will.

Sometimes, things go wrong because there could be errors of commission, meaning someone didn't fully comprehend a concept or didn't ask the right questions. And there could also be errors of omission, where something was done incorrectly or not done at all. The important thing is to identify what went wrong and ensure it doesn't happen again.

I observed an unfortunate situation where a marketing admin launched a text message campaign, but the internal coordinator running the campaign accidentally included the wrong link. Instead of directing prospective students to the application page, the link led them to unsubscribe. Yikes! The repercussions of such an error were significant and skewed our data. We didn't know if people who clicked wanted to unsubscribe or wanted to get more information.

To avoid these kinds of mistakes, the key is to slow down, double-check everything, and follow the old adage: "Measure twice, cut once." This rule isn't just applicable in carpentry; it's a valuable lesson for every professional, especially those starting in their careers. Rushing often leads to errors, and the effects of those mistakes can serve as early career lessons.

But what if you don't have a plan at all? Without a plan there is almost no way to avoid being a "short order cook." Operating without a plan makes it challenging to identify what's going wrong and where to go next. If you find yourself in a situation where things are going wrong and you don't know how to correct them, it might be because there isn't a clear strategy in place. That's why, if things are going off track, it's crucial to pause and establish a comprehensive plan before taking any further steps.

You don't want to be playing a game of whack-a-mole where you randomly try to hit anything that pops up. Winners of this game are typically those who watch the game, identify patterns, and strategically plan their moves. Those who react without a strategy tend to lose. If you're feeling this way with your marketing efforts, it's time to slow down, observe what's happening, develop a plan, and make more informed decisions.

3 PILLARS OF HIGHER EDUCATION MARKETING

Once given the authority to be strategic success driving partners, the process of moving from a reactionary marketing department to a strategic marketing department focused on enrollment can be difficult. Especially when ad-hoc requests were your norm. But luckily, thinking like a strategic chef is the key to these next chapters.

The higher education landscape is changing, with more competition and a dwindling number of potential students. Fortunately, the main parts of a digital strategy have remained stable and are likely to continue to do so, even if the details about how they are implemented change. And you can use this strategy to inform your institution's marketing plan.

To achieve success in a higher ed marketing strategy, you need to do three things well:

- Create an enrollment-driven website.
- Publish effective content that answers the questions prospective students and influencers are asking.
- Implement strategies to turn visitors into leads.

We will go into more detail on each of these three pillars in following chapters, but here is a basic overview of each.

1ST PILLAR:
AN ENROLLMENT-DRIVEN WEBSITE

Your website is the first and most important marketing asset you have. It is the first impression almost all prospective students will have of your institution. In many cases, this is where they will go to answer the big question: should I attend this school? But the biggest challenge is that your website has several audiences, including potential students, current students, alumni, faculty/staff, and donors. Yet you can effectively only focus on one primary audience.

Which is why the key decision you need to make regarding your website is who is your primary audience?

I would argue that the audience you should prioritize in designing your site is prospective students. As we just noted, your website is the most important point of contact with this group. If your marketing efforts with prospective students aren't effective, the other groups aren't going to even be there in the long run.

Once you know who your primary audience is, you can tailor your content to their needs. Why does a prospective student (or their parents, guidance counselor, or other influencers) visit an institution's website? What questions do they have in mind?

Bob Johnson, one of the pioneering voices in higher education website strategies, outlined three pivotal questions every student grapples with on one of our recent podcasts.[29]

Will I fit in?

Do they offer my desired major?

Is this institution financially feasible for me?

Keep in mind these questions could differ a bit depending on the type of institution and student demographics you are pursuing. But your site should at least answer the three questions above quickly and efficiently. This way, you can present a persuasive and emotional case for the student to take the next step of engagement (request info, visit, apply, etc.).

Take some time to audit your current site. Try to see it through the eyes of a prospective student. Does it answer these questions in a clear and compelling way? Does it present information in language that makes sense to someone who has never attended higher education school? If not, it may be time to revamp your site to make it more enrollment focused.

2ND PILLAR:
EFFECTIVE CONTENT

Content marketing is a powerful way to build your audience and connect with mission-fit prospects. It's helpful to think of content in two broad categories: top-of-the-funnel content and mid/bottom-of-the-funnel content.

At the top of the enrollment funnel are prospective students who haven't heard of your institution yet and may be early in the process of thinking through where they'll go. This audience has questions like, "What can I do with a bachelor's degree in computer science?" or "How do I pay for my schooling?" When you create quality, helpful content to answer questions like these, you attract organic search traffic from visitors who are in the broad pool of potential students.

This kind of content should focus on providing value and take a low-key approach to promoting your brand. If the content is successful, it will help new potential students become aware of your school and prompt them to find out more about it.

Bottom-of-the-funnel content is created for an audience that is aware of your institution and wants to learn more. Here, your focus is different. Instead of answering broad questions, you're answering specific ones like, "How does the program in computer science at [your institution] uniquely prepare you for a career in software development?" or "What scholarships are available at [your school]?" It is especially useful at this point to tell success stories from current students or alumni.

A good story is often a much more effective way to paint a picture of what your institution is like than simply sharing information. It connects with prospects on an emotional level and helps them develop a feel for your culture and values. Look especially for narratives that demonstrate career outcomes (how your alumni have benefitted professionally from their studies), personal transformation (how students have been changed during their years at your school), and the decision process (how current students made the choice to study at your school).

Many schools are so focused on showing off features that much of their content ends up being transactional. Meaning on a campus tour you promote that your library has 50,000 books instead of explaining that it's a place to rest, get away, and study. The key here is to focus on the benefits instead of the features. A website that looks like a college catalog with how much it costs per credit hour is a completely transactional website. And many of us in academia feel this is sufficient because we tend to focus more on the facts over connection. But if your website is full of helpful content that emotionally connects the reader to your school, you are selling the benefits and attaching your institution to their future success.

With effective content you can organically attract your key audience and teach them about your school. Talk about two birds with one stone!

3RD PILLAR:
LEAD GENERATION

Once you have an enrollment driven website and effective content, you need to start generating leads. There is some confusion to what a lead is, so let me clarify. A lead is when a potential student has interacted with your content in some way and provided contact information. This is the beginning of your relationship with them, and it is a relationship that may eventually lead to enrollment.

This part is obviously crucial. It is possible to have a decent website and lots of helpful content that attract organic traffic without making any connections. So you need a carefully-designed strategy for encouraging visitors to become leads. One aspect of this—which is often overlooked—is that you simply need to be intentional about asking.

Whenever you have a piece of content (for instance, an informational article or a program page), you should always include a clear call to action at the bottom offering a next step to the reader. Do you want your reader to find out more about the program, schedule a visit, or maybe get in touch with admissions? They won't know that unless you ask!

Another important part of lead generation strategy is to create lead magnets. Think of something that would be of value to your audience and then offer it in exchange for their contact information. There are lots of possibilities here. You could offer a guide, something like "How to graduate from college debt-free." Another possibility is a webinar. You might have a professor in your computer science department talk about the hottest jobs in tech right now and how to be competitive for them. These lead magnets should speak directly to your mission-fit student and help explain why your school is the best place for them.

Lead generation is an element of your higher education marketing plan that simply can't be ignored. When this is done well, it moves students down the funnel quicker and keeps your enrollment numbers where your institution needs them to be!

Each of these three pillars are important on their own, but they are designed to work in harmony. Focus your attention on doing each of these well, and they will enable you to successfully market your school both today and in the years ahead. Let's dive into strategy for each pillar in the following chapters!

PILLAR 1—ENROLLMENT DRIVEN WEBSITES

R ecent studies show that nearly all prospective students find your website critical in their decision to apply.

Which means you can't plaster information onto your site like a billboard and hope it is "good enough." You have to be intentional in its creation. Most website users judge your institution within 3.42 seconds based upon design alone.[30] That isn't much time to capture the attention of your mission-fit student. Every second counts. Wasting this precious time with information you *think* your mission-fit students want to know, instead of information they *actually* need to know, creates friction and stops them from choosing your institution.

I have worked on websites since they were just lines of simple text and a few pictures. In 1994, when I did my first website, there were not even content management systems, nor did CSS exist to format your text (anyone remember the <blink> tag?). This was back when creating something on the internet felt almost like conjuring magic. I was thrilled to be delving deep into the mysteries of the emerging World Wide Web.

Fast forward to the late nineties. During that time, I collaborated with bright interns from Anderson University to create tailored HTML forms to create a rudimentary content management system (CMS) for my clients to edit key content on their website. Fast forward to 2001, one of those interns, Ade Olonoh, now a recent graduate, had the idea to create a system that would drag and drop forms with ease. From that spark, he created Formstack, now one of the global leaders in form tools. I went on to grow Brainstorm, a top-tier digital design and branding firm in Indianapolis, where I was entrusted with helping giants like Motorola, RCA, and Lexmark with both digital and traditional deliverables. I've seen it all, right from the beginning.

And as technology developed, so did I. More and more the importance of a highly impactful and resonating site was drilled into me. When I created Caylor Solutions, I did so with all this previous knowledge and experience in mind and a dedication to helping academic institutions. My goal is to share my knowledge and give you marketing strategies that work. And one of the biggest things I commonly help my clients understand is the importance of building an enrollment-focused website.

Enrollment is the beating heart of revenue for every institution. When enrollment thrives, so does every facet of the school—from student services to alumni relations. It's simple: when enrollment does well, all boats rise. By honing in on enrollment, not only do you optimize resource allocation by avoiding the unnecessary media sprawl across departments, but you also ensure higher revenue inflow through improved enrollment numbers.

An enrollment focused website, with effective content (coming in Pillar 2) to support it, is the winning strategy many schools need to increase enrollment numbers.

3 CRITICAL QUESTIONS EVERY STUDENT SEEKS TO ANSWER ON YOUR WEBSITE HOMEPAGE

In Chapter 5, we talked about the three questions every student grapples with according to Bob Johnson.[31] As a reminder, here they are again:

1. Will I fit in?
2. Do they offer my desired major?
3. Is this institution financially feasible for me?

You can answer each of these questions on the homepage of your website.

WILL I FIT IN?

The higher education journey is about fitting into a new community. Prospective students yearn to know if they'll feel at home on your campus. They will likely mentally size up the student population compared to their high school or previous experiences. They want to know if your institution aligns with their beliefs, aspirations, and social needs.

A few ways to address this:

- Use authentic photography that showcases a diverse student life.

- Provide infographics detailing student demographics, perhaps showing the percentage of first-generation students or the geographical diversity.
- Highlight student success stories or testimonials.

Your goal here is to create social proof that the prospective student will fit in and find like-minded individuals on your campus.

DO THEY OFFER MY DESIRED MAJOR?

Yes, many students may pivot from their initial major during their academic journey. But at the outset, they are often fueled by specific aspirations, be it criminal justice, nursing, or engineering. Unfortunately, many institutions bury this crucial information deep within departmental pages, making it cumbersome for students to find. Which creates friction on their journey to find out if you are the right institution for them. Your mission-fit student likely isn't concerned about whether criminal justice falls under sociology or anthropology. They want a clear path to their career dreams.

To remedy this:

- Avoid structuring your website like a dense academic catalog.
- List out programs and majors in an easily searchable format.
- Prioritize the student's need for clarity over internal departmental hierarchies.

IS THIS INSTITUTION FINANCIALLY FEASIBLE FOR ME?

Navigating the terrain of higher education fees can often feel like a maze for prospective students.

Imagine a student enthusiastically considering your institution, but upon landing on your tuition page, they're confronted with an array of perplexing figures—from costs-per-credit-hour to seemingly astronomical annual tuition sums. While these numbers are crucial, their presentation often lacks context. Potential scholarships, grants, or discounts that can significantly alter the financial landscape are either hidden in the fine print or buried under layers of navigation.

Now, let's add another layer to this scenario. Behind many a student is a parent or guardian, financially vested and emotionally involved in this monumental decision. Picture a worried father or a budget-conscious mother peering over the student's shoulder at the computer screen. As they scan the page, their eyes widen, and a sinking feeling sets in. The high costs, combined with the labyrinthine presentation, might make them gently, or perhaps urgently, suggest, "Maybe we should look at other options."

To make the financial aspect easy to understand and navigable:

- Highlight the average costs of a degree.
- Offer the average cost after financial aid.
- Ensure your tuition page is transparent and user-friendly.

As we mentioned before, no one wants the price of a table in terms of cost per square foot; they want the bottom line.

Showing your price by credit hour is simply confusing and hard to understand for most who are not consistently in the higher education world. While your faculty and internal structures are vital, when it comes to website design, prioritize the student's perspective.

The modern student seeks transparency, relevance, and efficiency. They aren't likely to pick up the phone for clarifications. What they discern from your website will shape their perception of your institution. Make sure it's a favorable one.

TIPS TO BUILD YOUR OWN ENROLLMENT-FOCUSED WEBSITE

You might be thinking, this is great, Bart, but how do I create a website of my own? Here is a roadmap to help:

IDENTIFY YOUR FOCUS

Your website is for students, not the board. The board and administration, while holding integral roles in the institution, are not the primary targets of your marketing efforts. New platforms, designs, and trends may sometimes seem fleeting or irrelevant to some stakeholders but hold the attention of potential students.

While it's true that the dean and administration provide a structural and guiding framework for the institution, they might not always have their finger on the pulse of effective enrollment marketing. Typically, students make up 90% of net revenue for schools. It is essential that the website's design and content prioritize their needs and questions.

Stay student-centric in your approach. A school's website cannot be all things to all people. For years, you have fought the battle of everyone wanting their own space on the homepage. But when it comes down to it, how often are enrollment or donation decisions based upon access to the library or today's lunch menu from the homepage? Today's Internet users demand clarity. They also expect your website to serve their needs and answer their questions above all else.

Look to the titans of industry: Amazon, Walmart, Apple, Google. These companies have grabbed the advantages of the digital world—especially within ecommerce—to generate conversion and drive revenue. Education is driven by revenue as well. Determining your primary source of income (most likely enrollment) should help you focus your energies and provide a clear answer when faculty asks the question, "Why is my link not on the homepage?"

TELL YOUR STORY

Every campus has a unique story. While it's easy to see yourself as just one of many, every campus and every institution has its own offering, a specific benefit, and something that will cause the like-minded to gravitate to you when you share that compelling message. Spend time to discover what your brand is all about, and present it out loud and clear on your website.

In addition to writing about your story, have others tell your story as well. You can provide social proof by asking students, alumni, friends, faculty, and parents to give a testimonial about how and why your school is unique. Have them share their personal experience of how your institution impacted them. Use photos, vignettes, videos, blogs, comments, and other social aspects to get the message across.

Ultimately, you're selling an education made up of human experience and emotion. You are not selling buildings and fall foliage. Be sure that all of your photos, copy, videos, design styles, and general tone underscore and emphasize that unique brand aspect.

PLAN FOR 3 SCREENS

Today's websites are being accessed from mobile phones and tablet computers, as well as traditional desktop and laptops. The younger the demographic, the more likely they are accessing your website from a smaller screen. Planning for that experience is absolutely critical. Recent statistics demonstrate that over 55% of all websites are accessed via mobile device. Generation Z skews much higher.[32]

While one answer has been to develop mobile-only sites, that strategy typically ends up adding additional work and complexity to updating content. Instead, responsive website programming is the answer I would recommend. This style of web development assures that the user experience is optimized, regardless of the size of their screen, and allows management of the website to focus on new content and converting visitors, rather than constant changes and updates.

When planning for the three screens, don't forget about your other digital communications. Studies show that a large percentage of email is viewed via a mobile screen, so it's critical that responsiveness is also built into email templates and communications.

MAKE YOUR WEBSITE SCANNABLE

The days of simply surfing the Internet ended in 1999; today, instead of leisurely surfing, Internet users come to find specific information. You can take advantage of this. Shaping your website to be scannable and quickly answering your users' questions will provide a better experience and will encourage action.

Consider updates to your website that:

- Utilize lists and bullets
- Use headlines and subheads
- Employ best practices, such as having "Search" in the right corner and contact information in prominent locations on each page
- Short, simple paragraphs that are concise and deliver the message
- Use best practices for search engine marketing to assure that your granular information is found

Be sure that the organization and labeling of content is created with the website visitor in mind. While your institution may by organized in departments, your site visitor may not be familiar with that structure. Keep it simple for them to understand the majors you offer and to find the terms they need. Also consider the logical organization of content that is clean and clear.

DON'T JUST TELL

Traditionally, websites have been constructed of pages containing copy and photos—not much more than a typical printed brochure. But with broadband speeds, even on mobile devices, your website can deliver much more. Leverage your content to tell your story in a way that evokes emotion and response in your website users. Ask yourself, "What do I want my visitors to feel?"

To truly communicate your institution's uniqueness, be sure to create rich content and media. This can and should be in the form of video, infographics, animation, and illustration, in addition to traditional photography and copy. This media should be posted not only on your institution's website, but also through digital outposts such as social, video, and photo sharing sites.

The old medical school adage of "see it, do it, teach it" can be modified to "see it, do it, share it" for our social media culture. Consider your new content strategy to be that of "content nuggets" that tell the aspects of your story, but in ways that are easily shared and socialized among friends.

DRIVE TRAFFIC

Education websites historically have large numbers in traffic statistics.[33] Primarily, that comes from internal usage, athletics, admissions, and faculty.[34] But the key question to ask is, "Are my mission-fit students the ones viewing my content?" If not, how can you drive these potential students and their influencers to websites and ensure they are impacting the numbers?

Creating inbound marketing campaigns is the way to get in front of your key prospects. By identifying your audience and their habits, you can better create content and calls to action that will appeal to their needs. Look for inbound marketing channels through pay-per-click advertising (both search and social) and retargeting campaigns, including email and social media campaigns. Traditional advertising can also be a great inbound marketing tool when using tools to combine print and digital.

In all inbound marketing, it is crucial to set up individual landing pages with incentives and offers to entice the next step from your prospects. If you're driving parent traffic, offer a downloadable eBook on financial aid and how your school stacks up against others. If you're driving student athletes, be sure to have a landing page suited to their needs to grab their attention. Individual landing pages are the key to measuring success and repeating the process.

SET IT AND FORGET IT

Management of the website and content is one of the most demanding and thankless jobs. Keeping up with the requests, changes, and needs of a campus community can end up being a truly reactionary position and department, leaving very little time for strategic thought. As you contemplate your redesign strategy, look for ways to leverage integrations with other on-campus systems to reduce these requests.

Much of the detailed content that is needed on a website is often repurposed from other sources, such as course catalog, campus directory, event calendar, alumni magazine, and campus news. Look for ways to integrate these systems with scripts and programming to assure that changes from the registrar or other campus offices will be automatically reflected on your institution's website with minimum effort.

Through these integrations, the marketing department gains more time to strategically plan for projects that will impact enrollment, development, and other initiatives. Look for a partner that can assist with the integrations who can also help with the collaboration between marketing and IT. And, remember, today's website technology can be managed entirely by the marketing team. Most of the websites we create for our clients utilize tools that can be fully managed by non-technical, content-focused marketers.

BIG DATA

The new buzz is about big data and how to analyze the metrics you have to make better decisions. Websites can generate a tremendous amount of data, but you need to be sure you have tracking systems in place. In the planning of your redesign project, you should consider the questions you have about your users. Where are they geographically? What are they seeking? How are they arriving? Knowing these will help you better organize your website. This goes way beyond page views and unique visitors.

Once you have the data, tools will need to be in place to help you mine and extract the questions you have. Depending on the answers you seek, various off-the-shelf tools can be used to make refinements to your strategy. While you may not have the need or the tools to analyze the data right now, your future self will thank you repeatedly for designing your website and gathering the data today that will be needed tomorrow.

Start with the basics of Google Analytics. Add custom tools that define heat maps and click rates and be sure to use the data available from your social profiles as well as email and pay-per-click campaigns to build a marketing decision engine.

PERSONALIZED EVERGREEN INFORMATION IS YOUR FRIEND

The idea of personalization and evergreen content might seem like two opposing poles. But the integration of the two is vital for a dynamic web experience. Seems impossible to do both, right? In today's world, it's not.

Personalization is not just about addressing the user by their first name. It's about tailoring their online journey to feel exclusive and relevant. With advancements in web technology, you can even use an embedded code on your site to change the content based on the viewer's geographic location. A great tool I love is https://geofli.com/ (tell them Bart sent you). This means a student accessing the site from Montana could have a distinct webpage experience different than someone from Utah. It's like channeling the hyper-personalization one gets when browsing platforms like Netflix or TikTok, where content suggestions are tailor-made to user preferences.

This type of personalization is becoming an expectation from our users. If you haven't looked into these changes yet, I recommend you start. The power of this personalization is multiplied when used with evergreen content. Evergreen content means the content is timeless and perpetually relevant, even if the way it's delivered can be tailored to resonate with the audience's specific circumstances or preferences.

In a world of fleeting attention spans, giving your audience content that feels like it's "just for them" can be a game-changer. Blend that with evergreen content that remains valuable over time, and you have a website that's not only contemporary but also timelessly effective.

PILLAR 2.1—CONTENT CREATION

When defining "content," it is helpful to discuss what content is not. It is not filler. It is not words and images to fill pages or audio-visual noise to fill the silence. It shouldn't just exist to prop up something of real value.

Content—and especially great content—should have its own value. It should serve a specific purpose: to educate audiences who may have no relationship with you, to persuade them to learn more, to inform those who are already engaged, to elicit positive associations, or to solicit action. For all your content, you should look through this lens.

CONTENT CREATES BRAND AUTHORITY

Too many education brands assume people will listen to them because they are educators. But trying to educate without a

91

brand in place within a crowded digital landscape is like shouting into the void. Which is why you have to define, build, and defend your brand authority.

What exactly is brand authority? Forbes says, "...in conceptualizing a definition of brand authority, it's useful to think of it as a company's perceived expertise within an industry or topic. If the public accepts a company as a legitimate expert in their field, then we can say the company has brand authority. That being said, brand authority is not a status you can confer on yourself; rather it's a reputation and an element of trust that others must assign to you."[35]

I like how the author emphasizes the concept that brand authority is something you cannot "confer on yourself." It is a reputation and a trust that the public has given to you. Just like John Maxwell says, "He who thinks he leads, but has no followers, is only going for a walk."[36] These leaders have no real authority without followers. In the same way, brands that keep talking with no one listening are as ineffective (and annoying) as a toddler with a megaphone. They have no brand authority.

My quick definition of brand authority is this: You've got something relevant to say—and people are listening to you say it.

Two significant education companies, Chegg and Uversity, conducted a comprehensive study of high school students to understand how they were utilizing websites for their higher education search.[37] I found this report intriguing and decided to translate its findings into an infographic. I then published the infographic on my blog and discussed my interpretation of the data and its implications for higher education.

Fast forward to a year later, I was surprised to find my name footnoted in a book that I had stumbled upon during a routine Google search. Intrigued, I purchased the book, and to my amazement, I was referenced as a leading authority on the subject of the Chegg and Uversity study. The reason? My blog had ranked number one on Google for that particular topic. This ranking didn't mean I was more knowledgeable about the subject than Chegg and Uversity, who had commissioned and conducted the study. However, to the internet and its users, I had gained authority because I produced more content around the topic, making me the go-to source of information.

Curious, right? Internet ranking is not necessarily about degrees or accolades but about generating meaningful, engaging content. Educational institutions can use this principle to their advantage. They can create content that showcases their unique programs and the expertise of their faculty. By doing so, they become the "authority" in those areas.

Take, for example, smaller schools that have carved out unique niches for themselves, such as institutions who shine in music or nursing programs. They have firmly planted their flag by creating content that reflects their unique identity and ethos. By doing so, they have claimed their space and built brand authority around it. Some may not like the direction they take. And that is okay, because they are not that institution's mission-fit student. Niches such as art, dance, and engineering help define those "flags" that allow institutions to attract their mission-fit students.

When you plant your flag and create content around your unique selling proposition, you start to be recognized as an authority due to your consistent presence and relevance to the audience's needs and interests. The more content you produce across various channels regarding your unique selling proposition, the more your brand authority grows. You start to become the go-to resource for topics or products. When you consistently offer valuable insights and solutions and help solve the problems your audience faces, you reinforce your credibility and authority.

However, a word of caution: never claim authority you don't possess. There's a risk, especially in our digital age, of spreading misinformation or presenting oneself as an expert without the necessary credentials or experience. In the higher education industry, I've worked hard to earn my authority through the content I create—from blogs to podcasts, and now through publishing. This content served as the foundation, but it's my continued efforts that reinforce the authenticity of my expertise.

And let's not forget the importance of the watering holes. Just as animals gather at watering holes, so do prospective students and their families have places where they congregate— both physically and digitally. If you know parents are waiting in line at a high school to pick up their student, you could explore geofencing—a location-based marketing tool—to push ads to their devices. Understanding your audience's habits can help you create a multi-channel approach, using both physical and digital spaces, to reach your audience effectively.

Building brand authority in the world of higher education is a combination of consistent, quality content, claiming your unique identity, and meeting your audience where they are. It's not a one-and-done process; it's a continuous effort to engage, educate, and add value to your audience's lives.

When it comes to admissions content, some results are easier to measure (how many subscribers signed up for a tour?) than others (how well did we educate readers about our school?). But in all cases, great content should always be tied to goals. You can't always serve the end goal (enrollment) directly with content, but you can always serve smaller goals relevant to your ultimate goal.

PREPLAN YOUR CONTENT WITH A CONTENT CALENDAR

In Joe Pulizzi's book *Epic Content Marketing*, he says if someone is trying to sell you a one-time content campaign, run![38] These limited campaigns often have a strict beginning and an ending, which is why they don't work for continued outreach. A plan and program with an organic calendar far surpass sporadic stops and starts of project-based campaigns when it comes to getting your mission-fit students' attention.

Editorial calendars, content calendars, and social media calendars are the elements that should guide your marketing activities because these are the keys to regular and consistent content. Gone should be the days of asking, "What should I post on Facebook today?" That decision should have been made six months ago!

When you open your browser on Monday morning, your question shouldn't be, "What am I going to post on social media this week?" This approach is reactionary and lends to the chaotic churn of content production that feels endless and unproductive. It's also why many schools claim they don't engage with blogs; they're caught up doing the "short order cook" tasks rather than focusing on enrollment marketing.

When you have a content plan, it's like following a recipe. You know the ingredients, the steps, and the expected result. You've got a roadmap to guide you, and all you have to do is execute. Think about it like this: it's much easier to say, "I'm going to take one day to knock out six blogs because I know the topics, then I won't have to worry about it for another five weeks."

This strategy applies to all forms of content creation. For instance, I designate my Fridays from 12-5 for podcast creation.

Currently, I am about ten episodes ahead. Because of preplanning and creating a buffer, I don't need to worry about producing content every week. I never miss a week, even if I get "behind."

Proactive planning and efficient batching of work can save you from the madness of daily content creation and allow you to focus on what's essential—crafting powerful marketing strategies to attract, engage, and convert prospective students. But shifting your focus from a reactive to a proactive content marketing strategy won't be done overnight.

This journey will require a strategic plan to outline the milestones your institution will need to reach. I recommend you start with vision.

EMBRACE A SHARED VISION

I know this sounds a bit prosaic, but I cannot emphasize enough how important it is that every stakeholder in your content marketing efforts is on the same page. It is true for any organization, large or small, and it starts at the top with leadership.

Dr. Mark Jobe, President at Moody Bible Institute, said it best in our conversation on the *Higher Ed Marketer* podcast in 2022. "When I look at leadership, I have a limited responsibility. A good leader has to narrow down their primary responsibilities, and number one is clarifying vision."[39]

Above all else, higher education leaders need to ensure their school's vision aligns with their larger goals and objectives. Once you know how you're reaching your ultimate destination, your marketing team can successfully implement a long-term plan for delivering useful content.

What are the organizational goals that guide how you measure success? Some are quantitative:

- A target increase in traditional student enrollment.
- Similar increases in online, transfer, or nontraditional undergrad students.
- A certain amount of funds raised for the general fund (advancement focus).

Others are qualitative goals, or what you want prospects, funders, other audiences, or the general public to know about you:

- Your unique mission and vision.
- Your brand promise, or unique selling proposition (USP).
- Specific aspects you want to highlight, like campus life, graduate outcomes, etc.

Identifying what you want and need to say about your school is important. So is reviewing how you're already saying it. You'll likely find you have a lot of existing content sources (webinars, lectures, articles, etc.) you can adapt into blog content. But don't stop there! Remember your watering holes and use them. Your message will get ignored if you don't craft it to meet your audience where they are.

STRATEGIZE WITH PURPOSE

Once you've collectively outlined your vision, it's time to transform it into an actionable content marketing strategy. I touched on this already, but if you haven't done so, now is the time to identify your target audiences and their preferences:

- Who is your ideal mission-fit student?

- What are their needs, and how can your content answer their questions?
- What type of content do they like to consume?
- What are their digital platforms of choice?

If you want to engage with your audience effectively, you need to know who they are, what they are, and why they are who they are.

Start by developing a persona or two (or several) of ideal or target students. Give your persona a gender, ethnicity, occupation, household income, physical location, even a name. Consider what this person is thinking, seeing, doing, and feeling at the moment they're interacting with your content.

Why are these personas important? Because creating content with one person in mind is always going to be more effective than trying to reach everyone.

Next, brainstorm the questions this persona is asking at this stage before they've even heard of your school:

- What do I have to do to start my career in X?
- Where can I find a school that has Y?
- What's dorm life like?
- How do I pay for my schooling?

Notice the questions aren't "What programs does your school have in X?" That's a question your admissions team gets from active prospects (inquiries) already interested in you. Remember, we're out to reel in the ones who don't know yours is the perfect school for them yet.

In the fall of senior year (or earlier), students start making decisions about applying to schools. So it's a good time to answer questions about applying. Later in the fall, they are applying for FAFSA, so this is a great time to answer financial questions. Then, when they are starting to sign up for housing in the winter, that is a good time to talk about getting your dorm ready. Follow the natural enrollment pattern of a student, and you'll always have questions to answer on your site or blog. Even with young and adult learners, there are cycles they follow which creates a pattern you can follow, and your editorial calendar should note these changes. Don't get an order of Christmas toys in January! Give them the content when it's relevant.

After you've brainstormed your questions, it helps to spend a little time investigating how prospects are framing these questions when they type them into Google. Paid tools to assess search volumes and competition like Moz, SEMrush and Ahrefs are best. But don't sweat it if you're not ready to invest in those yet.

Other schools are using these tools to develop their Google advertising campaigns, and guess what? You can see what they're doing for free with the Google Keyword Planner tool.

Try typing in a featured program or topic you want to highlight. Discover:

- Whether Google advertisers are targeting those keywords.
- If so, their approximate search volume compared to other similar keywords.
- Their competitive scores (how hard it will be to get a page one search result).

Make a list of hot keywords. This will be a great guide as you begin to craft headlines for your content—those magnetic words that entice your target audience to click.

DEVELOP A CONTENT CALENDAR

A well-organized content calendar is a must-have resource in a proactive content marketing strategy.

Now is the time to get into the specifics of what type of content you want your team to focus on and to schedule publishing dates on target platforms. A good content calendar should also clearly delegate roles and responsibilities to your marketing team. By doing so, you'll optimize your resources and avoid last-minute scrambles because you forgot to schedule someone to write that Homecoming blog.

Figure out who's going to do what. It could be one person doing it all, but usually, it's a team effort.

- Writing—Research topics, adapt existing content, conduct interviews, create drafts.
- Editing—Check for relevance, suggest improvements, proofread, give final approval.
- Publishing—Selecting an image, uploading it to the blog.
- Promoting—Putting descriptive content about the post out onto social media to drive interest.
- Tracking—Reporting keyword rankings, traffic to the website, from the blog to other pages, etc.

If it sounds like running an online newspaper or magazine, it basically is! The main difference is volume. You don't need an "issue" full of stories every week or month. But as you adjust goals to make your content plan more robust over time—and you're seeing exciting results as you go—you may wind up publishing a lot more than you think.

Here are some examples of regularly scheduled content pieces and moments you'll want to focus on:

- Blog posts
- Social media posts
- Email campaigns
- Special events and key dates
- Admissions cycle phases

Don't forget your most valuable on-campus resource when planning for new content—your students! Pick their brains as much as possible.

Plan for as much content as you think you can handle producing and publishing in three to six months. Two per month? Weekly? Whatever it is, just prepare to be consistent.

Start basic. All each piece needs is:

- Well-written text (at whatever length it needs to be).
- At least one master image.
- A call to action that links the reader to additional resources about your school.

As a stretch goal, note in your calendar that one or two pieces of content in this initial period will be videos. Nothing too fancy. Just some simple visuals with a voiceover or on-screen text. Or you can even adapt a blog post into a Lumen5 video (a great tool I recommend looking into).

The whole point of a proactive content marketing strategy is ensuring your school gets the most bang for its buck from the get-go. That said, proactive marketing doesn't mean "set it and forget it." You still need to keep an eye on how your content is performing and make any necessary adjustments.

- Track Performance: Use every bit of aggregated data to track your content marketing metrics the second your content goes live using tools like Google Analytics.
- Collect Feedback: Ask your target audience for their honest thoughts about your content. You can do this indirectly through surveys and polls or directly through focus groups with current and prospective students.
- Stay Responsive to Changes: Adjust your plan when necessary. For example, ChatGPT completely altered the content marketing landscape when it went live in late 2022, and most schools should have adapted their strategy accordingly.

When used together, these methods will paint a picture of your content's effectiveness so you can refine it whenever your strategy needs to take a detour.

Planning in advance can feel like a chore, but the benefits are undeniable. It's the difference between running a marathon at a steady pace and sprinting in random directions hoping to cross the finish line. On my team, we put this philosophy into practice by planning our content twice a year. This semi-annual brainstorming session gives us the structure and direction we need and leaves enough room for flexibility and creativity.

When we sit down to plan, there's no sacred formula we adhere to. Sometimes, it's topics that have proven to be evergreen for us, ones that we haven't visited in a while. Other times, it's based on a presentation I've been working on or an idea sparked by a conversation at a conference. We also pay close attention to what's happening around us. Current trends and hot issues in our industry can be a goldmine for content ideas. Staying connected and responsive to the industry landscape keeps our content relevant and resonant with our audience.

Now, a final word of advice on putting together the content calendar: do not underestimate the power of details. When adding a topic to the calendar, leave yourself a nugget or two about the angle or point of view from which you'll approach it. This could be a sentence, a question, a statement, anything that helps you remember the essence of the idea when you revisit it. The trick here is to not strive for perfection. It doesn't have to be a well-fleshed out outline; think of it as a gentle nudge or a breadcrumb that leads you into the actual writing phase. Having these pointers in the calendar will make the transition from planning to execution much smoother and help prevent the dread of staring at a blank screen.

YOUR CONTENT SHOULD BE EVERGREEN

When I was eight, my great uncle, Ralph, gave me his collection of travel postcards. During the 40s and 50s, he and my aunt, Dot, traveled across the United States by car.

I have enjoyed these cards and the window of time they represent. But mostly I enjoyed seeing how different businesses used the postcards to market themselves. Most of the postcards showed color photos of the modern motels and travel stops. They acted as promotional works of art. But my favorite is the postcard for Canary Cottage Cafe. It's different from the others. It has valuable content marketing.

They provided a recipe for their chocolate fudge cake and fudge frosting. This additional content was not only useful and unique to the Cafe, but it also created an emotional tie with the restaurant and was truly "evergreen." The recipe didn't lose its value or relevance over time. And, it made the postcard intrinsically valuable, proving that the content itself added substantial value beyond the promotional aspect. I could make this same cake and fudge frosting 75 years later.[40]

This is evergreen content. It changes the ballgame and has value. I looked up the business location and found this small cafe has been replaced by a small office outfitter. But the usefulness of the postcard, the content itself, outlasted the business. If everybody could do that level of content marketing, they never have to worry about people forgetting them again.

That is true brand awareness—when people hold onto something because it has value, regardless of whether it's tied to you.

Evergreen content is timeless, always relevant, and continues to draw in readers long after it was initially published. One of the keys to creating excellent evergreen content is to focus on what people are searching for and focus on answering their questions. Jay Baer in his book "YoUtility" said, "Success flows to organizations that inform, not organizations that promote."[41] And he is right. People care more about themselves rather than who you are. You have to care about what you're mission-fit student cares about rather than trying to promote yourself.

The essence of evergreen content is in its longevity and versatility. It doesn't get stale, and it can be reused and repurposed in myriad ways, offering long-term value. For example, a podcast can be transformed into a blog post and further dissected into social media posts. Different content delivery vehicles can be utilized concurrently, while similar platforms, like blogs, may require a six-month gap for repurposing.

However, remember to periodically revisit, refresh, and double-check your content, ensuring links are functional and the information remains up-to-date. Even as you repurpose your content, you don't necessarily need to remove the old versions. By altering about 20% of the content, approaching it from a different angle, you can create a sense of authority and expertise around the topic. This clustering effect is recognized by Google, which subsequently boosts your page ranking!

For example, by creating multiple blogs around the theme of "higher ed marketing," I have reinforced my authority on the subject in the eyes of Google. Which in turn improved my Google ranking for that term. Don't let this term be general! Focus on improving your google rankings for terms that are specific to your niche. It's easier to market to a smaller, more targeted audience than a large one. If you identify your specific "watering hole," you don't need to appeal to everyone, just to those who align with your offering. Becoming more targeted can actually enhance the effectiveness and reach of your evergreen content.

To help you jumpstart your content creation, here are some ideas your school can use.

CONTENT CREATION IDEAS YOU CAN STEAL

TEXT-BASED CONTENT

Blog Posts

Blog posts stand as prime examples of highly discoverable content, distinguished by their helpful tone rather than the overt conversion intent seen in landing pages. To create content that resonates with your audience, consider a few tactics: ask your admissions team for common applicant inquiries, utilize a keyword research tool like Google's Keyword Planner to see what other institutions address, or brainstorm topics from your interactions with students. Cover a diverse range of topics—from campus life and mental health concerns for first-time students living away from home, to insights about the off-campus community.

The inherent broadness of your blog's content makes it ideal for a diverse audience. Your goal is to capture the attention of those searching for school-related content on Google, connections of your social media followers, and potentially e-newsletter subscribers. Make sure you disseminate this content widely, be it through a single post or a series.

Blog posts work because they have a propensity to be shared, referenced, and linked back to from other content, including content from other publishers. Take, for example, Gordon College, who to this day enjoys significant traffic for the keyword "Christian college experience" from their post "How Attending a Christian College Can Change Your Life," published way back in 2006. The lack of images doesn't diminish its relevance because the core strategy remains unchanged: answer real questions effectively enough for readers to reference and share your content.

Spotify

Spotify is an easy-to-use streaming music service that allows you to create and share playlists, effectively extending your marketing reach with a sprinkle of creativity. To get started, simply create a free Spotify account under your school's main email, like admissions@yourschool.edu. The content of your playlist could be tailored to various events throughout the academic year, such as a " School Name Move-In Favorites" or a holiday mix, making sure to highlight any musically-famous alumni. While you can share these playlists directly on social media, we recommend transforming them into a text-based content hub by featuring them in a blog post. You can integrate the music by right-clicking each song on Spotify, selecting "Copy Spotify URL," and embedding these links into your post.

The University of Wisconsin-Whitewater did this well with their blog post "Spotify Playlists for College Students." Notice they went above and beyond to publish playlists (plural) and used a plugin to display each playlist in a playable format. That's likely part of why this post from April 2018 continues to perform well in Google searches for "college playlists." This is highly discoverable content, ideal for attracting an outside audience both from social and search.

SAT/ACT Prep Tips & Tricks

The anxiety tied to academic tests, such as the SAT, is a real concern for many new students seeking to attend your institution, leading to a flurry of Google searches for tips and strategies. Tackling this through informative and helpful content serves not only the students, but also parents, teachers, and guidance counselors looking for resources to support them. This type of content, versatile in its nature, can range from a light, easily digestible blog post to a detailed white paper aimed at educators.

The key to creating this content is to make it a genuine resource that provides real value to your audience. Collaboration with instructors can lend credibility to an FAQ page or a more research-heavy piece. Remember, the aim here is not just to rank high in search results but also to send a message that your school is a nurturing environment, encouraging further exploration of your resources.

Take a leaf out of The Princeton Review's playbook. Their highly-ranked article, "3 Essential SAT Tips and Strategies," doesn't just stop at providing valuable information. They prompt visitors with a pop-up invitation to unlock all of TPR's content for free, simply by creating an account.

"What Should I Major In?" Quiz

Choosing a major is a major (ha!) anxiety point for incoming students and even their parents, who often worry about the potential repercussions of a wrong choice. You can help counter-act these fears through interactive content, such as a simple quiz. This isn't merely discoverable content; it's an ingenious way to build interest and guide students towards programs that could be a good fit for them, thereby increasing traffic to your program landing pages.

Interactive content doesn't have to be complex—it can be as straightforward as a text-based quiz with multiple-choice selections and an interpretation key. But there's room for creativity, as demonstrated by Goshen College's approach. They fed quiz responses into a visualization graphic, adding a layer of engagement as participants watched their results develop.

High-value content like this should be easily accessible on your website. Be sure to link back to it often in related content, such as blog posts, emails, and social media updates. After all, you will rarely find a better opportunity to pitch a program to a prospective student than after they've completed a quiz that tells them what could be a good fit.

Resource Page for Scholarships and Other Financial Aid

Create a guide on finding tuition assistance to help your students fund their journey to your school and reduce friction that might have kept them from your doors. I don't recommend you charge for this guide, but you should ask for an email address and some qualifying information in exchange. Rounding off the student anxiety trifecta is financial stress, joining the ranks of entrance testing and choosing a major. Creating content that not only promotes your institution but also outlines how to seek assistance from your financial aid specialists and points out resources students can independently access is crucial.

For a more comprehensive version, consider creating a downloadable resource—the more detailed your guide for finding money for schooling, the more likely visitors will be to offer their contact information to get it. This approach positions the guide as a great example of conversion content.

Grand Canyon University has successfully combined this approach with a paid search or pay-per-click (PPC) strategy. While it's not always necessary to pay to get your resource landing page to the top of search results for terms like "money for college," it's worth considering if your budget allows.

Application Process

As instructional content, the application process is ideal for sharing with an audience you have previously engaged with. The process of applying to any institution can be complex to the average applicant. Incoming students and their families want to know what to expect. This content should provide an explanation for how the process goes, step by step.

It works best as a page on your website made available to students who are already engaged with you as applicants. You can and should link back to it from any other related content. It serves to move interested prospects closer to taking the action you want them to take (like filling out the application form). It is not highly discoverable because, for a keyword like "college application process," it's difficult to compete with established advice sites like www.myfuture.com without investing in pay-per-click campaigns.

Testimonials

A testimonial is social proof content, which is among the most powerful you can produce. It enhances every other piece of content it touches.

Testimonials, coming directly from students, parents, and alumni, are goldmines of authenticity and versatility for your marketing strategy. They lend credibility to your claims and should be showcased prominently on your website, social media, blog posts, promotional materials, and more. The key is to stay as true as possible to the speaker's words, allowing their personality and enthusiasm to shine through. As powerful social proof content, testimonials significantly enhance the persuasiveness of your promotional efforts—according to OptinMonster, a site that helps convert website traffic to subscribers, 70% of people trust recommendations from real individuals, even if they are strangers, and this jumps to 92% if the person is a peer.[42]

Institutions like Anderson University (IN), Antioch College, and Lane Community College prominently utilize testimonials because they recognized their invaluable potential in enrollment marketing.

Alumni Magazine

A well-crafted, consistent magazine helps you maintain an open line of communication with your former students long after they've graduated. Through compelling storytelling, you can encourage your alumni to keep a steady interest in their alma mater.

Of course, drafting an alumni magazine strategy takes time and resources. It's also often one of the costliest lines in higher ed marketing budgets for schools that still rely on print. But by staying within a few basic guidelines, you can stretch your marketing dollars while still giving your alumni the messaging pipeline they deserve.

Now, there are two key points I'd like you to focus on for your magazine:

1. Your magazine's content should focus on answering your readers' questions.
2. A magazines with a regular cadence establishes authority by refreshing brand awareness.

It may be tempting to simply stuff your alumni magazine with self-promoting accolades about your institution. But your alumni want to be emotionally engaged by story-driven content, not dry advertising. Remember, your school isn't the hero of your magazine—your reader is. So, while they'll certainly care about their alma mater's wins, be sure to include information that will genuinely benefit them.

- Alumni successes: Put your former students' success stories front and center. Reach out to some of your prominent alumni on LinkedIn or put out a call to action for your readers to share their journeys with you.
- Exciting new programs: Digital technology is advancing faster than many of us can keep up. Your alumni will be curious to see what majors you're implementing to educate their future coworkers.
- Alumni engagement: Showcase stories of active involvement of alumni with your school, be it volunteer work or a guest speaking role.
- Your alumni's achievements and your institution's mission must remain linked in your magazine content. But ultimately, your alumni are the protagonists of the story.

GRAPHIC CONTENT

Prep Checklist

You'll get the most mileage out of this if you send it to a select group of alumni, high schools, and business leaders. Providing a tool to high school students to help them think through their next steps when preparing to come to your school is a great way to start building a relationship with them. A checklist takes what feels complicated in the minds of young people and presents it simply and succinctly. The message you're sending is: "You can do this," while strongly implying you'd like them to end up at your school.

A checklist can be as simple as a read-only web page or PDF, something a student can download and print! Though checklists can be gated downloads requiring an email address to access, unless bundled with added incentives such as exclusive coupons, they're not typically strong conversion devices. It's best to think of checklists as referral content geared more toward influencers than students themselves.

Transylvania University (in Lexington, Kentucky) has a fairly simple example of a web page organized around simple graphics, which they can easily link back to in emails and other strategic content. Cuyahoga Community College put together a nice graphic called Destination Graduation, intended to help students connect their educational path to life goals.

Infographics

When you have a complex idea to explain, or when you want to tell a story based on a collection of data, it's best to present this content visually. Text and tables in black and white just don't cut it anymore. Your audience will both take more interest in the subject matter and retain the information better if you present it as an infographic.

Depending on the subject matter, infographics can range from basic presentations using a reusable template to custom, highly detailed and ornate visuals. Know the value of this content product and use it accordingly. If it's a few numbers presented in a venn diagram, use it as part of a blog post and move on. A dated post is especially appropriate for blog posts if the information is subject to change. However, if your infographic is researched, detailed, and timeless, give it a prominent position on your website.

Infographics are versatile tools that can enhance discoverable and instructional content by quickly distilling information for an audience with fleeting attention. Whether persuasive or informative, they can entice newcomers or guide an established audience. For instance, Brandman University used an effective infographic to detail the process of becoming a teacher in California. Additionally, schools don't need to custom-make all their infographics. Private institutions, for example, can leverage resources from organizations like NAICU (National Association of Independent Colleges and Universities) to advocate for private institution quality and affordability, provided they properly attribute the source.

School Comparison Chart

With a little competitor research, you can make a strong case for attending your

school based on any number of factors that are best expressed visually. Start by

choosing your metric, or metrics: cost, acceptance rates, graduation rates, number of internship opportunities, etc. Identify your top competitors, hit up their websites, and record the data. But don't stop with a simple (boring) table. Make all that hard work pay off with a chart that pops!

A compelling comparison chart, preferably placed on your website's admissions page, is a powerful tool in promoting your institution. It's also effective when shared over social media, where proud students and alumni can amplify its reach. Such charts not only showcase your school's strengths but also serve as social proof of the sharer's positive experience, fostering a sense of school rivalry. Whether your unique selling point is lower tuition, like The College of Davidson and Davie Counties, or something else reflective of your brand, the inclusion of contact information and a call to action ensures the chart serves its purpose effectively.

Budget & Financial Aid Calculators

When creating content, you can reasonably assume the prospective student is thinking seriously about higher education and is looking specifically at the affordability of your school. With a calculator, you can give the prospect an estimate of your tuition so they can build a realistic budget and feel confident they know what they're getting into.

This is another piece of high-value content that should go on the admissions page of your website. Link back to it in all other content about cost, preparing for next steps, discussions to have with family before leaving for school, etc. You want lots of backlinks to this because it is useful and gives you a great call-to-action opportunity. Ask users to contact the admissions department with this information in hand, and offer to answer their financial aid questions. And remember, don't require personal information to use your calculators. As an engagement tool, you want the interaction to be barrier-free.

The more attractive, useful, and interactive your calculator, the better example

it is of conversion content. A good place to start for calculator ideas is finaid.org. You'll find lots of basic calculators for cost, savings plans, loans, budgeting, etc. Design your calculator to prompt the applicant with brief, simple questions in an attractive format. Williams College has an elegant Cost Estimator tool worth taking a look at for inspiration.

eBooks

Blogs are great places to present a single, useful idea or touch on a list of ideas. But for more complex concepts, a detailed list of multiple resources, research- or interview-heavy information, or any subject matter it will take you days rather than hours to research and present, an ebook is often a better format than a blog post. It should be far more graphics-driven than a blog post as well.

The best use for a new ebook is as a gated downloadable file. Present it on a landing page and require contact information for access. Then, promote that landing page heavily according to your campaign goals and budget. When your campaign is over, however, you can use it in other ways. For example, you might move it to a library of resources that is more organically discoverable than a landing page. This is definitely a good move after you have produced your next new ebook. You'll want to focus promotions on the new material.

Ebooks serve as excellent conversion and instructional content with wide-ranging applicability. They can be incorporated into information packets for prospects, repurposed into smaller blog posts, or used in printed form during personal interactions with applicants. Their timeless nature ensures lasting relevance, as demonstrated by Indiana Wesleyan University's "10 Tips for Navigating Financial Aid & Scholarships," which continues to be a valuable resource for their admissions department and an enduring marketing tool, flexible for different formats and updates.

VIDEO CONTENT

Application Explainer

One of the simplest videos you can produce, an application explainer takes applicants through the process of filling out your school's online application. The idea is to remove any uncertainty in the applicant's mind about the nature of the questions. With this video, you're letting them know in advance what questions they will need to be prepared to answer. This can be as simple as using a common screencast recorder program with a microphone.

The video, which you might title "How to Fill Out an Application to [Your School]," should have a prominent position on your admissions page. Embed it so the video is playable without the need for download or the use of a video player. The easiest way to do this is to upload the video to YouTube and use the embed link on the webpage, which provides the added benefit of content discovery on YouTube, the world's second largest search engine.[43]

As instructional content, videos like this help tip interested prospects over the fence by demonstrating the ease of this critical step in the application process. It holds their attention long enough to encourage them to take that next step. The University of the People understands this, which is why they included a video in addition to a written explanation of how to complete their online application.

FASFA Tips

Some important content that would work okay as a text-based product can also come across as pretty dry, which may leave it unread. A good strategy to overcome this is to strip the dry content down to its essentials and present it as a video. Content about the Free Application for Financial Student Aid (FAFSA) is a good example of this. More applicants will watch a short video about a government form than read a detailed article about it.

A FAFSA video is content valuable enough to include on your admissions website, but with interest for a broad enough audience that you can use it everywhere else as well. It's great for social media, email, presentations to visiting groups, materials to provide schools, etc. Virtually every student is interested in this topic, no matter what school they are thinking about attending. By putting your video out broadly, you'll create awareness which you can then steer toward your school website.

Because "FAFSA" and related keywords are such popular search terms, your FAFSA video will make a great addition to your discoverable content arsenal. Texas Wesleyan University nailed it with their "Filling Out the FAFSA 101" video: it's relatively short, sticks to the essentials, and has solid production value. In short, they've succeeded in presenting a dry topic in a relatively entertaining way

How-To Applied Science

Your content should present the value of your school in a variety of ways: a path to success, a supportive environment, a prestigious alumni network, etc. Those are all strong messages. But don't forget to tell them that yours is a fun and exciting learning.

These are especially effective with a STEM focus. Capture your science, technology, engineering, and mathematics students applying what they've learned to a cool project and show your audience what they're missing.

These fun, infinitely shareable videos, ideally published on social media, are superb discoverable content. As the fun factor escalates, so does the sharing and the recognition by Google that your content is valuable. Concurrently, they make for powerful referral content, winning you influential advocates as you build affinity around STEM-related subjects. By targeting high school science teachers with whom you have a relationship, you can encourage them to share this content with their students. You can see a great example of this from Fanshawe College. Even without ample time or budget for detail, the key is to create a sense of something cool happening and enticing prospects to join in.

Virtual Tour

Your campus is one of your school's biggest distinctives, and it doesn't take a physical visit to show it off. Virtual tours are interactive video (or multiple-image) content that provide the next best experience to being there. They can be done using a custom tool that may or may not be in your budget. The simplest option is to upload 360-degree photography to Google Maps. By doing this, you vastly expand what images Maps users see when clicking on your campus beyond Street View. Your images can include foot traffic only areas and the view from inside buildings that effectively allow users to go on a self-guided virtual tour.

By leveraging Google Maps, one of Google's most popular tools, you can substantially increase the visibility of your campus. After uploading your photography, embedding the Google map onto your webpage becomes a breeze. This functionality can also be utilized to create a virtual tour video, by simply record-ing a screencast of yourself navigating through and panning the images.

Once published on your admissions page and shared on social media, the added 360-degree images enhance your campus's discoverability in local searches due to Google's prioritization of Maps results. And, if you opt to create a video, it doubles as an instructional asset! Virtual tours are an excellent way to address applicants' questions about campus life, and following the visual impression of their potential home, it's an opportune time to encourage them to fill out an application form or schedule a physical visit. Check out our work with Franklin College, Indiana, to see an example!

Campus Safety Video

Safety may be a top concern for some students, but there's no question it's a topic parents are interested in. That's why a well-done campus safety video has value beyond checking a compliance box during orientation. When made available externally, it gives the traditional applicant's number one influencer peace of mind. It shows them your school is a place that takes prevention of theft, assault, sexual assault, and other crimes seriously.

Remember when we say "well-done," we don't mean high budget. It only needs to be well-written with confident line delivery, high-definition picture with strong lighting, and disciplined editing. The simplest use is as a YouTube video, easily embedded in communications to referral organizations or parents who have requested information, and easily shared over social media channels.

Brown University's campus safety video has gotten thousands of hits since 2012, and every viewer has been treated to a creative presentation of safety tips along with plenty of shots on-site at its beautiful campus.

YouTube Channel

According to Pew Research conducted in 2022, YouTube is now the #1 social network for Gen Z.[44] This is something your school should take advantage of. Especially because it is easy to feed all of the above content into your school's YouTube channel.

It's best to think of your channel as its own piece of content, a collection of organized videos that together tell your school's story. If you have enough video content, you might categorize them under separate sub-channels, perhaps by department. Give your best videos a prominent position on your YouTube homepage by making them Featured. Then, plan to publish content regularly (e.g. once a week) and purposefully (according to a strategic editorial calendar that aligns with your overall digital marketing campaign).

When your channel is (or channels are) in place and you have set up an editorial calendar, you can begin asking viewers to subscribe to your channel. That makes your video content far more visible, as your channel is added to the user's subscriptions list. If they choose, they may receive alerts and email notifications of new content you publish as well. It's a good idea to begin including a call to action at the end of your videos, asking viewers to subscribe and/or comment. Just be sure to assign someone the task of monitoring comments and responding to any questions users have about your school.

Video is increasingly the most discoverable content type, and YouTube reigns supreme as the top publisher of online video content. That means treating YouTube like your video blog (or "vlog") will bring far more attention to your school than a text-based blog alone will. It takes work, but a strong video strategy creates unmatched opportunities to engage with a broad audience and ask them to build a relationship with you. It's why Biola University has gone all-in with YouTube.

DIGITAL CONTENT

Texting Campaign

Content written for this platform is ideal for nurturing the attention of prospects and applicants (as well as current students) who have opted in and alerting them to new information. Text content could include a thank you note for attending an event, inviting them to the next one, asking them to take a survey (with a link provided), reminding them of upcoming application deadlines, and much more. Content might be specific to your type of school. Christian institutions could send out daily devotional content, for example.

Using a third-party text messaging service like TextMarks, TextUs, or Trumpia allows you to directly engage with prospects who have opted in. Simply input your content and monitor the results. This approach is highly effective due to the immediacy of text messages, with 82% being read within the first five minutes! However, be careful not to overwhelm your audience with excessive calls to action to avoid opt-outs.

The ultimate goal is to convert recipients into attendees and applicants. Check out Tri-County Community College's well-structured signup page which clearly outlines the opt-in and opt-out process and includes a privacy policy—an important aspect to discuss with your school's legal counsel.

Email Nurturing Campaign

As opposed to an email blast, which simply goes out to everyone on your email list, a nurturing campaign is targeted to individuals based on some specific action they have taken. Many enrollment departments call this "communication flow." It often starts with a trigger. If a potential student attended an event, you send them content related to that event. If they fill out an application form, you send them content that explains what happens next.

These flows are crucial in holding the attention of a select audience and guiding them through specific actions. This process can typically be automated in a Customer Relationship Management software (CRM) such as Slate, Salesforce, or Element 451, or third-party email services like Constant Contact, Emma, or MailChimp, which transitions the applicant's email address back to the general list once the desired action is completed. Nurturing emails are often more impactful than general email blasts, and they signal to prospects that you value them and are committed to their success, serving as excellent conversion content.

Clarks Summit University has set up numerous nurturing campaigns, where prospects completing certain actions receive personalized emails, encouraging a deeper relationship with the school. These nurturing practices significantly increase the likelihood of prospects taking further actions towards enrollment.

Parent's Email Newsletters

Messaging is always most effective when targeted, and it's never a bad idea to target parents. A parent blog is an excellent place to publish pass-along content designed to spark conversations between parent and student. Parents want to partner with you in encouraging their students to succeed, and they want to be kept in the loop with regard to family events. But you can't expect them to feel informed just by posting content to a blog. It's important that you get into their email inboxes as well.

Whatever content you publish, make sure you're emailing it out regularly and in a timely manner. Regular contact with a prospect's parents—weekly, ideally—is important for keeping them engaged. And they need to be timely with regard to any upcoming events or deadlines. Be sure to give parents plenty of time to act or to talk to their student beforehand.

Parent-focused content is essentially the perfect referral content. There is often no stronger influencer in a student's life than a parent, and no more important partner with your school in the admissions process. This is why our client Indiana Wesleyan University remains committed to pushing out their post content to the parents segment of their email list after setting up their parent blog.

3D Printer File Download

3D printer files offer a unique, inexpensive method of engaging prospective students by enabling them to create branded items, such as keychains or smartphone cases, themselves. Most high school students who are already engaged with STEM might have access to a 3D printer, so as part of your marketing strategy, you could upload a STL file for them to use.

Currently, it's more common for schools to publish their 3D printing policies, then direct visitors to free STL download resource sites (e.g. thingiverse.com). But there, visitors may find knick-knacks with the brand logos of other schools. This is a missed opportunity! Instead, they could upload an STL file to a site like thingiverse.com, then provide a link directly to it from your library's page (or a STEM-focused landing page) and promote the free STL download with *your* branded knick-knacks future students can 3D print themselves.

PHYSICAL CONTENT

Laptop Stickers

Is a sticker "content" or just branding? It all depends on what you do with the medium. A sticker with your school's logo on it is a good branding tool. But when you start thinking of items like this as a physical canvas for short-form content, you can use them to deliver a meaningful message. You can turn current students into brand ambassadors while you're at it.

This is a great tool for in-person contact, so you'll want to give these out at events. You can also employ student ambassadors to use and hand out your laptop stickers. Current students are especially effective at connecting with high schoolers in person.

Any content on display in physical spaces makes for good discoverable content, at least in the traditional sense. But it also functions well as referral content because of the way it facilitates conversations. Olin College of Engineering worked with an agency to create laptop stickers with three connected hexagons (reminiscent of gears or molecules). Each bore the logo and an identifier: Volunteer, Donor, and Continuum Club. It's an effective way to deliver the message that "I'm invested in this school" while provoking questions like "What's the Continuum Club?"

Another approach is to work with your department of campus safety to develop branded stickers that identify registered laptops. The University of Michigan's stickers declare the device is "registered and traceable," an excellent theft deterrent. This communicates something about your school many students might not have thought about it, but appreciate when they see it: your school takes thrift prevention seriously.

Dimensional Mailer

With a little creativity, mailers can provide recipients with a delightful experience. Dimensional mailers accomplish this by presenting content in all three dimensions. The recipient may open a card to see the building where they'll pursue their degree pop up in the center. Or, they might pull folded paper out of a pouch to discover it pops itself into a gift box. Inside might be a promotional code for a free t-shirt. The possibilities are endless. Whatever your actual content, you've gotten their attention with the delivery.

Because dimensional mailers are a more significant investment than standard direct mail, you'll want to save this tactic for a big enrollment push. Segment your mailing list as best you can and develop as many personalized versions as your budget allows. You might have three versions targeting prospects who have indicated interest in STEM, fine arts, and business, for example.

Something as simple as a poster in a tube—like the one my son received from Huntington University a few years ago—begs to be opened. And if you include an invitation to a fun event, chances are good your prospects will see it and respond.

Pet Mailers

It's direct mail that's not "for" the prospect. Instead, this content is "for" the dog of
the house (or the cat). The idea is to build a sense of alignment with pet owners while addressing a common concern

about going off to school. Your prospects are going to miss their pets! If you can demonstrate you understand that with some playful content, you'll definitely have their attention.

Like dimensional mailers, this works best (and is most cost-effective) when targeted to families you know have pets. This isn't the kind of thing you send out regularly to the same recipients, because the joke can get old. Include these as part of a big enrollment push. Dogs and cats are part of the family in over 60 million and 47 million U.S. households, respectively. Their "support" means something on an emotional level.

That's why Butler University put their mascot, Butler Blue III, on a postcard.

He wrote a letter (well, dictated—humans did the typing) to the house pet indicated on the prospect's application. Blue put the dog of the house at ease about their human going off to school. In another version, he made peace with the cat to enlist its help. Butler's admissions folks knew if they could make their pet-loving prospects smile, they were building relationships.

Each one of these ideas are proven, and you see them in action in the examples I've listed. I hope you steal them and utilize them for your own school. Especially because—once again—you do not have to reinvent the wheel! But you do have to pick an idea and decide how to shape it towards your specific mission-fit student.

PILLAR 2.2—CONTENT MARKETING

Now that you've got content created, let's discuss how to use it.

The American Marketing Association (AMA) defines content marketing as "a technique of creating and distributing valuable, relevant and consistent content to attract and acquire a clearly defined audience—with the objective of driving profitable customer action."[45]

Well said, right?

The core of your content strategy should be to inform, educate, and inspire, which then triggers a following and encourages action. This action could be enrollment, filling out a form, or setting an appointment with your admissions team, but the action itself should be clear. By addressing the concerns and curiosities of your audience, you not only cater to their needs but foster trust. And that trust turns into an opportunity to get them on your campus.

But understanding your audience is only half the battle, it's why we have a 2.2 chapter when it comes to content. Because the content alone isn't enough, you need strategy as well. Your content needs to reach its mission-fit student, so becoming discoverable is a high priority.

This is why content marketing is hard for many. They don't regularly put out content, and they don't look for ways to solve problems. The content they do put out typically only informs instead of inspiring solutions, leaving the masses feeling unheard and uninformed.

Content created this way is sadly a waste of time. I know how busy you are, so this chapter is full of the principles I've shared with institutions across the nation to help them grow their enrollment numbers and get found by the right students.

CONTENT MARKETING IS FUEL

Think of content marketing as gas for your car. Without it, you're not going anywhere, no matter how flashy the vehicle is. It's the juice that powers your social media and the magnet drawing visitors to your website.

Recently, I had the pleasure of hosting Brian Piper, coauthor of *Epic Content Marketing, Second Edition*, on the *Higher Ed Marketer* podcast.[46] While his book isn't strictly about higher education, its lessons are universal. It reminded me of an often-overlooked truth: the practice of content marketing isn't new. Ever wonder where the term "Soap Operas" comes from? They started as emotionally charged, dramatic radio shows, which were sponsored by brands like P&G and Ivory Soap. [47]

The goal? To sell more soap, of course! Content marketing in its early days, right?

Flashback 25 years, and the chatter in the boardroom would be all about splurging on big-ticket advertising. A spot in the Super Bowl commercials? Golden. But today content reigns supreme.

Sadly, many businesses don't realize this. They're still trying to light the fire without any wood, underestimating the volume and variety of content they could (and should) be using. Remember, in today's saturated digital space, everyone's vying for attention. How do you rise above the noise without breaking the bank on a Super Bowl ad? Killer content. If you want to be discovered, invest in content.

Even when big commercials were all the rage, companies like Procter & Gamble were looking for ways to connect with their audience. But they hit a home run in their 2012 Olympics campaign where they pulled at heartstrings with their "thank moms" campaign. It was a brilliantly emotional advertisement, recognizing mothers as the pivotal supporters behind many athletes. There wasn't a dry eye in the room. Since then, P&G moved away from highlighting unique product features to focusing on narratives that foster a genuine connection with their audience.[48]

The idea of creating content to connect deeper with your audience isn't new, but it is more important than ever. If you only advertise features and price, it is a race to the bottom and becomes a question of how much money you have to spend to outbid your competitor. Instead, you need to do something outstanding and out of the norm and get people talking about you organically.

So the big question is: how do you create content that compels your audience to take action?

The beginning of everyone's search on the Internet begins with a question. When users go to a search engine, they literally type in the question they have in their mind. Then, the search engine attempts to find the answer.

If you can identify the questions your audience has and then answer them within the content you create, search engines will find you and send traffic to your school's website. SEO really is that simple—but it's just not always easy to pull off. Instead of asking the questions our audience is asking, we are tempted to ask questions that revolve around our own interests like the following:

- What new programs do we have?
- What awards have we won?
- What is our vision for the future?
- How are we going to solve the problems in education?

These questions are organization-centric, not audience-centric. If your content is answering these kinds of questions, your web writing will suffer poor conversion rates and you won't properly fuel your marketing goals. The best thing you can remember is every piece of content should be *interesting* and *helpful* to your mission-fit student, not to your boss or your board.

DISCOVERY VS DESTINATION

In content marketing, two dynamics are critically important: positioning yourself as a destination and ensuring your content is primed for discovery.

Consider an institution renowned for its expertise on Shakespeare. And because of this, the institution is sure to regularly post Shakespearean content. With time, this content could gain significant attention, making the institution a destination for Shakespearean knowledge.

But just being a destination isn't enough. This content also has to be easily discoverable. For instance, when someone searches for insights on a Shakespearean sonnet and stumbles upon your content, it should be well-optimized and authoritative so you can transition from being a search result to a trusted destination for that individual. If you do this right, that individual will likely follow your website just as they would follow an account on their social media feed that aligns with their interests because they anticipate more of the same quality content.

Today's modern content creation services a dual audience: human readers and digital algorithms. We need to structure content that caters to both without compromising its value for human readers. This is where search engine optimization (SEO) comes in. Tricky, I know, but if you get your content right it will be easily discoverable by digital algorithms while remaining substantive and engaging for human audiences.

Search engine algorithms are the behind-the-scenes digital detectives who play a pivotal role in deciding which content gets highlighted and which gets buried in search results. It's crucial to note that while keywords are an important aspect of SEO, they are not the end-all-be-all. Gone are the days when "keyword stuffing"—the practice of cramming a web page with keywords to manipulate its search ranking—was effective. In fact, search engines now penalize this behavior. Modern SEO is a sophisticated dance that balances keyword relevance with content quality, user experience, backlinks, and other factors.

Merely inserting a keyword repeatedly into an article will not only annoy human readers but can also get you in hot water with those ever-vigilant search engine algorithms.

On the other hand, your human readers are in search of authenticity, relevance, and engagement. They want content that speaks to them, answers their queries, or ignites their curiosity. And while optimizing content for these algorithm criteria can increase discoverability, it shouldn't be at the expense of its value to the human reader.

As content creators, our goal is to bridge the gap between the binary language of algorithms and the rich tapestry of human experience. The synergy between these elements is crucial. There's a saying in the digital marketing world: "The best place to hide a body is on page 2 of Google." Because, let's face it, few people venture beyond page 1 of Google.[49]

Educational institutions possess a unique advantage in this arena. I've observed schools who have initiated a monthly posting schedule and witnessed a notable improvement in their search engine rankings in as little as four months. While a brand new business might take 2-3 years to achieve similar traction, educational institutions are already a step ahead. Thanks to the .edu domain extension, search engines already regard schools with a degree of authority. This inherent trustworthiness is a significant leg-up in the world of SEO.

The formula is relatively straightforward: generate blog posts that directly address the questions your target audience is asking. This strategy not only offers value to your readers but also positions your institution as a responsive and authoritative source of information for SEO.

WHERE SHOULD CONTENT BE?

Everywhere.

Websites, social media, blogs, videos, stickers, and even chalk drawings on the sidewalk. But if you want to know where to put your content, pull out your phone and look at the apps on your home screen.

Most of your content will be accessed on a mobile device. The more you look at where you consume content on your own phone, the more you'll understand where you should be putting content. But don't stop there. Content should be omnipresent. While it's a given that platforms like websites and social media are prime spaces for content, don't confine your creativity to just these realms. Content, after all, is a versatile tool, capable of leaving an impression anywhere, from the virtual space to the physical world.

In recent years, innovative marketing methods have stretched the boundaries of where content can reside. Take vehicle wraps, for instance. What was once just a mode of transportation, an RV, or even a golf cart, can now be transformed into a moving canvas of content. A couple of decades ago, institutions might have simply sought a golf cart in school colors. Today, thanks to advancements in printing, those same carts can carry messages, stories, or calls to action while moving around the campus.

Limiting content to the typical trifecta of blogs, websites, and social media is a missed opportunity. Institutions willing to venture outside conventional channels, to integrate content in both digital and unexpected physical spaces (chalk drawings, graffiti, tattoos, etc.) are the ones poised to truly harness the power of content marketing. Content is universal, and its potential applications are only limited by imagination.

In a crowded market, where countless institutions are vying for the attention of potential students, the trick isn't just producing content, but positioning it in a unique space where your competition is minimal. This is about crafting a niche, about prioritizing discovery in places where your mission-fit students frequent, rather than just following the pack. While the allure of trending marketing methods can be tempting, you should evaluate if it genuinely resonates with your target audience. The question isn't whether a billboard or magazine ad works, but if it works for *your* mission-fit students.

Be a unicorn, not a lemming. The lemmings might all be rushing in one direction, but as a unicorn, you have the power to stand out, to captivate and draw people towards you because of your distinctiveness. Don't get boxed in by conventional wisdom. Every institution has a unique story and audience, and your content strategies should reflect that. Step back, assess, and dare to disrupt the status quo with your content.

A NOTE ON VIDEO CONTENT

YouTube is currently the #2 search engine in the world,[50] yet many marketers shy away from creating video content because they don't have the setup to create high quality video.

Guess what? You don't have to have an expensive setup to create a high quality video. Likely the smartphone in your hand could take video in 4k quality, which actually rivals certain professional cameras. Anyone with a smartphone can easily step into the world of videography.

However, the power of a smartphone goes beyond its technical prowess. The authentic feel that smartphone-shot content delivers often resonates deeply with younger audiences. Generation Z, in particular, has grown up amidst influencers, vloggers, and social media platforms where content is candid and direct. For them, a video's authenticity can often hold more weight than its production value. Overly polished and refined content sometimes runs the risk of appearing disingenuous, especially to an audience that values raw and relatable material.

To further enhance the quality of smartphone video content, a few strategic investments can prove invaluable. A quality microphone, specifically designed for smartphone usage, can elevate audio immensely. Meanwhile, a simple tripod can lend the desired steadiness, making videos appear more professional. And, the charm of natural light should never be underestimated. The soft, diffused light streaming in from a window can often outshine elaborate studio setups in creating visually appealing content.

At the heart of any video, regardless of the tools used, is the story. The landscape of video content creation is evolving, with authenticity emerging as its reigning champion. Budget constraints don't need to get in your way when it comes to creating engaging videos. With creativity, genuine storytelling, and leveraging the tools at hand, impactful and engaging video content is well within your reach.

DON'T FORGET TO REPURPOSE

Have you ever played with Legos? The pieces are varied, yet each holds potential. Individually, they may seem insignificant, but when assembled, they can form complex structures, from simple houses to intricate castles.

Such is the nature of content.

Each piece, like a Lego block, can be reimagined, reshaped, and repurposed to create something new, yet familiar.

Content creation doesn't need to be a laborious task of consistently inventing the wheel. Instead, you can reimagine existing content to cater to different audience preferences, ensuring its reach is as widespread as possible. The beauty of repurposing is that it embraces the diversity of consumption habits. Not all audience members digest information the same way. While some may lean towards a podcast during their morning commute, others might prefer to cozy up with a comprehensive ebook in the evening. Repurposing ensures that the same essential content is accessible in a myriad of ways.

For instance, a podcast episode can spawn a detailed blog post by transcribing its content. Such a post, with the addition of other related writings, can then be compiled into an ebook. Taking it a step further, that ebook could even be expanded into a full-fledged book. On the shorter side of the spectrum, distinct points from the book might inspire engaging carousels on social media or get condensed into an informative infographic.

At its heart, repurposing content is a strategic approach. It's the art of asking: "Now that I have this content, how can I reimagine it? How can I ensure it reaches the right eyes and ears? Through which platforms and tools can I deliver its message?"

#HASHTAGS ARE YOUR SECRET WEAPON

A few years ago, my wife and I took our family to Disney World for the first time. Upon arrival, we registered and each of us received a large button that proclaimed "1st Visit" surrounded by Mickey, Pluto, Goofy, and Donald Duck. Our family was so excited, we promptly pinned the buttons on and set out. I didn't think much about it at the time, but throughout our week-long visit, that button worked magic.

Whenever we were waiting for attractions or walking down the streets, characters and other Disney staff members would seem to go out of their way to ask us if we were having an enjoyable time and if we needed anything. Only later did I realize those buttons were the signal for others to engage in an intentional way with my family to ensure we had a good time and increase the chances we would come again.

Just as Disney World uses the power of a button to encourage engagement with the right audience, your social media strategy can do the same. Rather than a pin to wear on your apparel, you have the power of the hashtag to get you and your message noticed.

According to "X," formally "Twitter," a hashtag is "any word or phrase with the # symbol immediately in front of it."[51] Hashtags were created organically by Twitter users to organize the vast amount of content that continuously flows through the social media channel. Besides organization, hashtags also make it easier for users to follow a conversation about a specific topic, or to find information on a topic.

According to Readwrite.com, the first hashtag originated in 2007 with Chris Messina on Twitter to bundle conversation around the upcoming BarCamp global technology unconference he helped fund.[52]

Since the hashtag's introduction on Twitter, nearly every network uses them in one way or another, including Facebook, YouTube, LinkedIn, Instagram, Pinterest, and other social media platforms. Suffice it to say, hashtags are here to stay. Choosing hashtags is an important process in your strategy, and you should find tags that are in circulation to associate with your organization by using tools like hashtagify.me. Plus hashtags make you more discoverable. Many Twitter users leverage the hashtags in their profile descriptions for this reason.

Another reason to leverage hashtags is to gain the attention of influencers. Within the Hashtagify.me toolset, you will get the ability to identify the most influential users for a particular hashtag. This is important because every time an influencer retweets or engages with your communication, it will be amplified to their audience—and to possible followers for your organization.

Indiana University leveraged hashtags as part of a brilliant admission promotion. The simple use of the hashtag #IUsaidYes on bright, bold red envelopes produced a viral social media campaign when students began posting selfies with their acceptance letters. You can use them to build your audience and your school's overall brand.

7 SECRETS TO CONTENT MARKETING SUCCESS

SECRET #1:
USE SIMPLE, EVERYDAY WORDS.

It's not demeaning or condescending to use simple words. It is a courtesy. This secret often feels counter-intuitive for academic staff, who are used to reading unbiased, unemotional, and impersonal content daily. I understand that for us in the academic community, simple words just don't feel professional. But if you think of your audience and what they want your web content to do for them, it makes complete sense. Even a PhD doesn't want to consult her dictionary while browsing your alumni web page. Simple, casual language is a must for powerful web writing.

SECRET #2:
WRITE IN SHORT SENTENCES.

Short sentences keep eyes moving and fingers scrolling. This doesn't mean you can't use conjunctions. But don't use them too often. Too many conjunctions make your reader feel like the sentence never ends, and they'll probably stop reading.

And yes, your English department faculty will object, stating that the website doesn't reflect the quality of the education that the prospective students will receive. Gently remind them that you are creating marketing content, not writing a dissertation. Both have very different purposes.

SECRET #3:
LEARN TO APPRECIATE "WHITE SPACE."

"White space" is the empty space in a design.

It is the equivalent to open, fresh air for the eyes. If you jam your page full of words, or squash them together into dense paragraphs, your reader will feel crowded and hesitate to read your copy.

White space gives clarity to the text and guides your reader through it. And this is getting more important as more users are accessing your site via mobile browsers.

How do you create white space? Write in short paragraphs. Paragraphs should ideally not exceed two or three lines.

SECRET #4:
WRITE FOR INTERACTION.

Web copy should be interactive. Place hyperlinks, buttons, and clickable banners in your text whenever possible so your reader can dive further into your website's content. Hyperlinks will also improve your SEO.

Another way to increase interaction with your content online is to allow comments on your blog posts. Let your audience share what they're thinking and ask you questions. In a similar vein, stay active in your social media threads and groups!

Keep the conversation going so they stay engaged with your content. One more thing. If you link to a landing page, make sure the headline copy and content of the landing page is directly related to (even repeating) the content they clicked on to get there. Your visitor won't stay long on the landing page if they're confused by the headline and content of your landing page.

SECRET #5:
START WITH THE MAIN POINT.

Journalists have been using what they call "The Inverted Pyramid" technique for a long time to catch the eye of readers who're scanning through news headlines.

There's a lot calling the reader's attention in a newspaper, so if the journalist wants his article read, he's got to catch the reader in the first paragraph. So, he writes the big, juicy parts of the story at the very beginning instead of burying it deep in the story.

This technique works brilliantly on the web. Your audience is swimming in an ocean of content. Don't make them dig to get to the best parts of your content. Entice them to read further by keeping your main point highly visible in the lead.

I also recommend writing subheadings every so often to keep your audience moving or skimming through your content.

SECRET #6:
EXPECT YOUR AUDIENCE TO LAND ANYWHERE ON YOUR SITE RANDOMLY.

Web writing is not like novel writing where readers read through the chapters in order until they arrive at the climactic ending. In the digital world, visitors land on pages at random—like opening a book in the middle and starting to read.

Successful web writing repeats key brand phrases that highlight your education brand distinctions across every page, blog post, ebook, or other type of content. It assumes that your brand distinctions are new to your reader, that they haven't been anywhere else on your site yet.

You should also take every natural opportunity (don't force it) to point the visitor to the main content pillars of your website, like your homepage.

SECRET #7:
USE RICH CONTENT.

Design, copy, and rich media should work together in harmony. Audiences expect a rich, immersive, and visual experience when they come to your website.

Make sure you write copy with these visual elements in mind:

- Quote bubbles
- Callout bars
- Featured images
- Photos dispersed throughout the text
- Testimonial or explainer videos

This isn't an exhaustive list of all the visual and interactive elements available on the web, but this is the foundation of rich media—and it is just as important as the words on your page.

CONTENT MARKETING METRICS

Metrics and measurements aren't just numbers; they're the heartbeat of your content marketing strategy. When done right, they give a clear picture of your successes and areas for improvement.

You could be dedicating countless hours to content creation without actually making headway towards your goals. You need to measure your audience's reaction to what you put out there. By analyzing their behavior, you'll quickly know if your content is hitting the mark or missing it altogether.

While you don't need to track every single metric, there are certain key performance indicators worth noting:

Website Engagement Metrics:
- Pageviews: The number of times your content's been accessed.
- Sessions: Each individual visit counts.
- Bounce Rate: Indicates the percentage of one-page visits.
- Users: This highlights unique visitors, differentiating from repeat ones.
- Time on Page & Pages per Session: Gives a sense of your content's stickiness and overall site engagement.

SEO Analytics:
- Impressions: When users spot your ad online.
- Average Position: How well you're ranking compared to competitors.
- Backlinks: Signifying trust and authority, these are external links pointing back to your site.

Social Media Metrics:
- Reach: Measures the span of your content's visibility.
- Engagement: Beyond likes, this tracks deeper interactions.
- Click-Through Rate: Analyzes engagement beyond the platform.
- Follower Growth: Monitors the organic growth of your community.

Once you're familiar with the metrics you'll be monitoring, it's goal-setting time. Use past data if available or make an informed guess if starting from scratch. Remember, bigger institutions might have loftier goals, but smaller entities should aim for consistent, steady growth.

Content marketing is a dynamic field. It's natural not to hit every goal on your first attempt. But that's okay. The primary aim of metrics is to guide growth. Whether it's amplifying site engagement, bolstering brand visibility, or boosting enrollments, the point is to progress. When the numbers hint at a misstep, that's your cue to pivot and adapt.

Instead of feeling lost in the digital marketing maze, let metrics light your path. There's immense relief in moving from gut feelings to data-driven decisions.

LOOK OUTSIDE YOUR TEAM
FOR CONTENT CREATION

Not everyone should create content. Some on your team or in your institution may be good at it, and others might not be. But you don't have to look solely within your own team for content creation.

Surprising as it might be, campuses often overlook faculty as potential content contributors. Their expertise and unique perspectives can make your content stand out. Don't fret about them being too busy; technology can simplify content collection. For instance, they can verbally answer a few questions via tools like Reverb and your team can then turn their answers into engaging content. And don't forget your student creators. They might have a significant online following. Collaborate with them to tap into their audience.

If you need to extend your content capacity, freelancers and marketing agencies can be your go-to. They add value without the commitment of permanent hires. If no one on your team is good at creating content, consider this strongly! It is worth the cost and often allows your team to spend more time on what they are good at.

Lastly, don't overlook the power of content curation. In July and August, big box stores like Ikea, Target, and many others are generating content around how to decorate your dorm room and the 10 things you need to go back to school. They use content marketing to highlight their products, but if you share this content, you are curating useful information for your students. You didn't have to create the content, but your audience found it helpful and now knows they can look to you to help them find useful content during these times.

By sharing content from major brands and media outlets, you are not claiming a partnership, but you are aligning your institution with trusted brands to provide your audience with useful resources. When done right, it positions your institution as a knowledgeable guide in the higher education journey. As you share external articles or tips, prospective students and parents perceive you as a trusted source. They believe you know what they need and are providing them with the best resources out there.

You can even take widespread issues, like the nursing shortage, and link it back to your institution's programs. By sharing such an article and highlighting your nursing program's high graduation rate, you are not just curating—you are connecting. You are illustrating how students at your institution can be a part of the solution while getting into a high security job.

Remember, content, without a content marketing strategy, isn't enough. You need to create relevant content, then put it in relevant places for your mission-fit student to find. Only then can you sit back and enjoy getting noticed.

PILLAR 3—LEAD GENERATION

First, let's define lead generation because I see many marketers get this wrong.

At its core, lead generation is about gathering a list of individuals who have shown some level of interest in what you're offering. It usually includes at least names and emails. Yet, many institutions often believe that simply drawing visitors to their website is effective lead generation. This is brand awareness, not lead generation. Increasing web traffic is an achievement, but if you aren't actively capturing details of those visitors (such as name and email) that you can then follow up on (with an email campaign), then you're primarily involved in a brand awareness campaign, not genuine lead generation.

With lead generation, you have tangible names and contact information you can directly engage with.

Years ago, when marketing was more general, lead generation strategy was straightforward and easy: broadcast your message

CHASING MISSION FIT

wide and far, and hope someone hears and responds. It was similar to trawling for fish with a wide net spread behind the boat. You don't know what you might catch, but you'll likely catch something. Now, with so many channels available, and the overwhelming amount of information that bombards individuals daily, this approach isn't as effective. Especially for smaller institutions with tight budgets.

Modern lead generation requires a more targeted approach. Much more like a fly fisherman using a rod with a specific lure. You are not trying to appeal to everyone; you are looking for those mission-fit students who align best with your institution. And there are three specific ways these students are likely to find your institution.

THREE WAYS STUDENTS WILL FIND YOUR SCHOOL

#1 LEGACY

Legacy students hold a special place in the heart of any educational institution. These are students who have a familial connection to the school—perhaps their parents, grandparents, or aunts and uncles once walked the same halls. They arrive on campus with a sense of familiarity and tradition, and they often have a deep-rooted emotional attachment to the institution.

But today, institutions can't depend on legacy students like they once did. Though the legacy connection is powerful, it's not as prominent as it once was, meaning schools can't depend on legacy students to fill their halls. But, your institution can still maximize this connection.

Strategies to Engage Legacy Students:

- Personalized Touchpoints: Moments matter. If a legacy alumni has a significant life event, such as the birth of a child, don't just acknowledge it in the alumni magazine. Send them a branded onesie. Then, make a note to follow up in 15 years. You can reach out again when their child starts high school and send preparatory materials for your institution, subtly hinting at the tradition.
- Alumni Partnerships: Form a strong relationship with the alumni office and set up a process which notifies you anytime a major alumni life event occurs. It could be winning an award or even launching a successful business. Send them a congratulatory gift expressing how proud your school is to see them succeed.

Alumni are not just for donations. If you implement the strategies above, you'll maintain a deep connection with your alumni, which will then influence the children they have towards your school. Instead of continuously reaching out for donations, build a rapport.

The philosophy should be: "How can we first earn their trust and friendship? Then, when the time is right, discuss support and donations." When I served on my alma mater's alumni council, we were often reminded we were in the business of "friendraising" and not "fundraising."

#2 INFLUENCE

Throughout the higher education decision-making process, students look to significant figures in their lives for guidance. Whether it's a teacher, a close friend, a coach, or even an admissions counselor, these individuals often sway the choices made by prospective students. Historically, schools rooted in faith enjoyed a steady stream of students recommended by church leaders, mainly because many of these schools were an extension of particular church denominations.

However, the rise of the internet and countless educational opportunities mean that these traditional pipelines have become less direct. Today's students often find their fit without the immediate influence of religious or community affiliations.

But even if traditional church leader influencers are less prevalent today, other influential figures still play a vital role. Coaches, mentors, or even peers can guide students towards a specific educational institution. Sometimes, this influence is the natural outcome of genuine relationships; other times, it's the result of intentional efforts made by schools to foster influential ties.

When I was a student, I had a summer job where I would go out and represent my institution at several youth summer camps. We would drive all over the country to these camps wearing school colors and giving out swag. We went with only one goal: build relationships with the youth at these camps so they would want to come to our school. My school wanted us to become influencers to these students so they would remember their institution when it came time to pick one to attend.

To genuinely harness influencer potential, you need specific marketing tactics tailored to these key individuals. They are often gatekeepers to the mission-fit student you seek. Here are a few strategies you can use.

- Building Relationships: Begin by cultivating relationships with influential figures in high schools or youth groups, such as program directors or youth pastors. This could involve creative gestures like inviting them onto a podcast or delivering surprise treats like coffee and donuts.
- Deepening Trust: Once the relationship is established, build trust to gain better access to mission-fit students. This can be done through email campaigns or presenting to their groups.
- Involving the College Community: Consider initiatives like "college takeovers," where existing students visit schools or groups to share their positive experiences.
- Hosting On-campus Experiences: Encourage high schools or other youth groups to hold events like band camps on your campus. During such events, don't just limit your presence to a promotional table. Engage directly, fostering positive experiences and memories associated with your institution. If your school already rents out your facilities during the summer to other organizations for band camps, sports camps, etc., be sure to actively be involved with enrollment marketing regardless of the ages of the groups. Younger students are often more impressionable than those who might better fit your short term goals (such as rising juniors or seniors).

The key is to remain top of mind for these influencers so when they think about higher education, your institution is the first place that comes to mind.

#3 DISCOVERY

Discovery is about being where your prospective students are and presenting them with relevant, timely, and memorable information in ways they'll appreciate and remember.

If a student types "best college in California for photojournalism" into their search bar and is led to your institution, they are likely to look deeper. They'll explore your website and content, look at how much it costs, and if they fit into your campus more so than if you enticed them to your website with free swag. Which is why showing up in page one of Google's search rankings is so important.

Unlike yesteryears where billboards and print media were the primary discovery channels, today's students are navigating their choices through search engines and digital platforms.

You can up your discovery efficiency by:

- Leveraging Search Engines: The power of organic search (like crafting blog posts optimized for relevant search terms like "Best nursing program in Utah") can drive considerable traffic to your institution's site.
- Tapping into Social Media: The lines between discovery and influence often blur on platforms like TikTok. An influencer mentioning or sharing an experience about your school can spark interest among their followers, turning a passive viewer into an active seeker.
- Thinking Outside the Digital Box: While online platforms are invaluable, in-person guerrilla tactics can create memorable impressions. The impact of a local institution's RV turning up at a high school

football game and distributing hot dogs and informational pamphlets will stand out more than ads among all the digital noise.

To truly harness the power of discovery in today's digital age, institutions need to foster a sense of relationship. Instead of relying solely on large-scale marketing campaigns, schools should aim to connect with potential students on a personal level, providing them with tailored information and creating meaningful interactions.

Now, with the knowledge of the three likely ways students will find your school, you can apply practical lead generation methodology.

PRACTICAL LEAD GENERATION METHODOLOGY

Lead generation is how you keep the doors open and enrollment numbers up. It is the third pillar of higher education marketing because it's best achieved once you have pillars one and two standing. From there, you can begin applying these tactics.

SEARCH ENGINE MARKETING (SEM)

I call this section SEM, because SEO in and of itself shouldn't be your only focus when trying to land on page 1 of a Google search. It isn't just about splashing cash on pay-per-click campaigns. It starts by truly understanding your audience, their queries, and their needs.

Everything in search engine optimization (SEO) begins with the user's question. Engineers have specifically designed search engines to pull up web pages and media that it believes to be the most relevant and quality answer to the question of the user. This means that if you want to rank high on the list of websites in a search, more than anything else you need to be answering the questions of the user.

This, of course, isn't the whole of search engine optimization. But without it, any other thing you do to optimize your website for search ranking will fail.

Of course, you can also pay to get your website ranked higher, but relying heavily on this strategy doesn't work out for higher education marketers. When you push your way to the top through paid advertising, you run the risk of attracting students who have questions that you are not answering. When this happens, you hurt your rankings because potential students quickly navigate away from your site (i.e., increasing your bounce rate). This tells the algorithm your site isn't helpful and shouldn't be high on Google rankings. It also hurts your brand image by disappointing the users who visit your site.

The best SEO strategy in the long run is designed to boost your organic search ranking. Organic search rankings are unpaid, natural rankings that are the result of the search engine's algorithms. Using an organic strategy means that you focus your efforts to rank high in a search by providing the very best answers to the questions that relate to your organization. When you build each page with this end goal, every page has the potential to rank high in search engine results.

And, the users who click on your links in the search results page are likely to get the answer to the question they were asking, which increases your brand strength by providing a quality experience for the user. When this happens, you'll have higher quality traffic from search engines, and the users arriving at your site from search engine results will be more likely to be in your target market.

CONTENT IS KING, BUT CONTEXT IS QUEEN

Google's algorithms have evolved, focusing on authentic, people-first content. But that doesn't mean one can ignore the technical intricacies of SEO. There's a fine balance between crafting quality content and ensuring technical optimization.

Every single page, from program details to contact information, is content. And you should approach website design with content as a priority. Quality trumps quantity. It's not about producing volumes of content but ensuring that the content genuinely addresses the needs and queries of potential students.

Search engines like Google and Bing prioritize websites that are frequently updated, so posting new blogs consistently is a fantastic way to make Google your friend and rank high on search results pages. You can post once a week, or once a month, but whatever the frequency, you need to stay consistent.

PAID VS ORGANIC LEADS

The great debate in the world of digital marketing has always been between the allure of instant paid campaign results and the sustainable, yet slower, rewards of organic strategies. For schools, this debate is critical, given the stakes involved in student recruitment and enrollment.

Paid leads come from advertisements or even people selling lead lists with hundreds of potential student names and contact information on them. Here, institutions pay to have their content positioned strategically, hoping to catch the eye of potential students. On the other hand, organic leads originate from unpaid sources. When a potential student types in a search query, and your institution's content appears naturally due to its relevance, that's an organic lead. And organic leads often convert at higher rates because the discovery is rooted in genuine interest and not just ad visibility.

Organic leads have other advantages that schools should seriously consider. These organic leads tend to have greater longevity. While setting up a solid base of organic content takes time and effort, the content becomes an asset that continues to attract leads long after its creation. Unlike paid campaigns that dry up the moment you stop investing, organic content has the potential to be the gift that keeps on giving.

Paid advertising has its place, but you should be wary of creating an over-reliance on it. The digital landscape is continually changing, with algorithms and AI dictating the rules of the game. Schools that place all their bets on paid strategies could find themselves at the mercy of these unpredictable shifts—meaning algorithmic tweak could render an ad ineffective overnight, leading to unexpected dips in visibility and engagement. Focusing solely on paid campaigns is like building a mansion on rented land. The space isn't truly yours, and its benefits are fleeting. But truly organic content provides long-term security and returns.

A blended approach often works best, especially in the initial stages. Launching with both pay-per-click and organic initiatives can provide the immediate visibility that institutions crave while laying the groundwork for sustainable organic growth. Then, as the organic content begins to gain traction over time, schools can strategically reduce their reliance on paid ads and shift towards a predominantly organic approach.

GUERRILLA TACTICS

Adhering strictly to traditional marketing norms can leave institutions lost in the crowd. To truly stand out, they have to be unconventional, innovative, and often surprising. But this doesn't come easy for higher education institutions.

Using guerrilla tactics means stretching the imagination beyond familiar boundaries and viewing challenges from fresh angles. Traditional marketing paths are well-trodden, and while they offer the comfort of predictability, they often lack the spark needed to captivate today's discerning and digitally-savvy youth. The goal here isn't to follow; it's to lead, and to sometimes challenge the very rules that institutions believe bind them. This could mean creating a viral challenge, organizing a flash mob on campus, or running a social media campaign that humorously flips academic cliches on their head.

Adopting such tactics isn't always comfortable, but the most impactful strategies often reside just outside one's comfort zone. Not every idea will resonate with faculty or administrators—and that's fine. What matters is that these campaigns resonate with prospective students. Overthinking, a common trait in academic settings, can be the bane of guerrilla marketing. Over-analysis leads to hesitation, dilution of innovative ideas, or even complete paralysis. Risk is inherent in any innovative venture, and staying in the safe lane rarely leads to groundbreaking results.

Be bold and memorable. Try new things, even if you fail at them. You'll discover something new about how to better speak to your mission-fit student.

With AI, brainstorming has taken on a new dimension. AI tools can be a goldmine for out-of-the-box ideas. By feeding an AI system an innovative concept, coupled with details about the target audience and asking it for more creative ideas, schools can get a plethora of guerrilla tactics tailor-made for their institution. It's the merger of technology and creativity at its best.

TRADITIONAL TACTICS

Think of the swag-laden school fairs where stickers fly off the table and eager students jostle to grab branded pens. These methods still work, but we need to change them up so they don't feel stale. Traditional doesn't have to mean predictable. Instead, the aim should be to push the envelope, even within tried-and-true frameworks, to create a unique and memorable impact.

For instance, fairs often come with a set of guidelines, including the types of giveaways institutions can offer. For one of these events I attended, I wanted to give out branded coasters, but the regulations limited giveaways to items like pens and a few other stationary objects. What did we do? We created costcards! These were branded coasters printed on thick cardboard—technically still in the realm of paper—which just barely allowed us to adhere to the rules. But, the costcards were distinctive enough that they were a fan favorite.

Another area ripe for reinvention is apparel. T-shirts have long been crowd-pleasers, but what if you added a QR code on the back? Imagine students waiting in line at an amusement park, their eyes drawn to the intriguing QR code on the shirt of the person ahead of them. Curiosity piqued, they scan it, leading them straight to your institution's website or a specific campaign. By integrating technology with traditional swag, you're tapping into today's digital-first mindset.

Incentive-based campaigns are another arena where the classics can get a fresh makeover. One institution I worked with offered a $500 scholarship to students who visited the campus and took the typical two-hour campus tour. But they weren't getting much interest. So at the next fair, we created a sign that said "Earn $250 an hour—ask me how!" Talk about an attention grabber! Suddenly we had student after student asking us what that meant and filled up the campus tour slots for weeks to come.

By approaching these classic strategies with a creative mindset, institutions can ensure their campaigns remain relevant, engaging, and effective. The key lies in the twist.

REFERRAL CAMPAIGNS

Your alumni are more than just former students; they are your institution's most passionate advocates. Their time at your school has shaped their lives, and many harbor a deep sense of gratitude and pride in their alma mater. This makes them invaluable assets in promoting your institution, particularly through referral campaigns.

Alumni don't get involved in referral campaigns for one simple reason . . . they aren't asked!

In fact, too often alumni are only asked for money and nothing else. It's not that they're unwilling or indifferent. On the contrary, many alumni would be thrilled to contribute to their school's growth and reputation. The issue often lies in not being proactive in reaching out and not providing clear, actionable steps.

A generic request like "recommend students" may be too broad and can lead to inaction. A more effective approach is to provide clarity. For instance, instead of a vague ask, you might say, "We're keen on students who excel in arts and humanities. If you come across such talents, please hand them this referral card."

By providing context and specificity, alumni can more easily identify potential students, making the process less daunting and more actionable. They will often jump at the chance to promote their alma mater, especially when given clear guidance on how to do so.

Remember, if you never ask, the answer is always no.

IDEAS FOR IRRESISTIBLE LEAD GENERATION

Lead generation isn't just about gathering names and details; it's about offering something of value that resonates with your target audience in exchange for those details. Whether it's a quiz that helps them discern the right major, or an invitation to a roundtable discussion with other prospects, the goal is to provide tools or experiences that aid their journey to your school.

Think of gated lead generation content as the secret sauce that can help "level up" prospective students on their higher ed journey. If they pay a simple price for entry, like giving their email, you'll grant them access to these invaluable resources. And this content could be as simple as a fun interactive quiz!

What's important is that prospective students believe your lead generation content provides them with legitimate value. Only after you establish your authority on their specific needs will they be willing to reciprocate that trust and build a relationship with your school.

The best part about lead generation content is that you have several workable options available to you. Here are some types I've seen provide positive returns for many of the schools I've worked with:

- Case studies
- Ebooks
- Infographics
- Quizzes
- Templates
- Webinars

That said, many higher ed marketing teams have enough on their plate. So I've pulled together a healthy list of practical lead generation content ideas for you.

Case Studies

Case studies are impactful pieces that showcase authentic examples of your student success stories, and I highly recommend you include them in your front-end content.

However, there are still selective opportunities to grab a lead's attention with genuine empathy storytelling:

- "The Benefits of an X Degree: A Real-Life Story"
- "A Diverse Community: A Student's Story"
- "How I Earned My Online Degree While Working Full-Time"
- "Why Our Alumni Keep Coming Back for More"
- "A Comeback Story: How a Campus Embraced a Struggling Student"
- "How Student X Solved X with Their Research Breakthrough"

E-Books

Ebooks are a great way to summarize much of the content you've curated on the front end of your content marketing strategy into one convenient place.

You can use them to offer leads to a one-stop shop for many of the answers they're looking for rather than jumping around from page to page on your website. I provide a similar service at Caylor Solutions, like my Marketing on a Shoestring Budget ebook.

Here are some handy ebook ideas for lead generation content:

- "The Must-Have Budgeting Guide for College Students"
- "A Beginner's Guide to Online Learning"
- "5 Practical Study Habits for College"
- "How to Keep Your Work-Life-School Balance Balanced!"
- "Campus Life: What You Can Expect as a Dorm Resident"
- "10 Online Tools You Should Use in College for 20XX"

Infographics

Infographics are often companion pieces to other types of lead generation content. However, if you have fully fleshed-out visual content at your disposal, then by all means, put it to work!

These are a great way to simplify complicated data and make it easily digestible for inquiring prospects with appealing illustrations. Consider partnering the appropriate visual content with one of these topics:

- "A Visual Guide for a Healthy College Lifestyle"
- "Breaking Down College Majors and Careers"
- "Small vs Large Schools: What Size Fits You?"
- "The Science Behind Study Habits"
- "Top 10 Points to Consider When Picking a School"
- "Essay Writing: What Matters and What Doesn't"
- "Getting the Most out of Online Study Resources"

Quizzes

Quizzes are such a flexible tool. Of course, you can apply them in the classic sense to give prospective students feedback on their competency levels.

Hopefully it goes without saying that these quizzes should be fun and engaging, not rigid tests like the ones your prospects will take in the classroom:

- "Think You Know Everything About Financial Aid? Find Out Here!"
- "What's Your College Study Vibe?"
- "Which Majors Match Your Personality Type?"
- "Curious Which Student Club Is Right for You? Take the Quiz!"
- "Think You've Got an A+ Budget? Let's See if You Make the Grade!"
- "Want to Study Abroad? This Quiz Will Help You Find Your Dream Spot!"
- "What You Need for Your Dorm Room and What You Don't!"

Templates

Whether for financial aid requests or job resume prep, templates can save your leads tremendous time and energy.

By offering templates for areas like academic endeavors, career advancement, and financial planning, you can showcase your school's willingness to invest in its students' success at every level:

- "7 Resume Templates for Soon-to-Be Graduates"
- "Write a Winning Scholarship Essay with This Template"
- "Your 20XX College Budget Template"
- "Your 10-Step Guide to an A+ Research Paper"
- "Build Your First-Year Fitness Plan with This Tool"
- "A Time Management Calendar for Students on the Go"

Webinars

Webinars are interactive virtual gatherings that allow prospective students and parents to learn more about your school's brand and offerings through live engagement.

They're an excellent opportunity to demonstrate your school's faculty, programs, and facilities in a dynamic setting.

Your school can use them in your lead generation content strategy by promising a seat in one of these exclusive webinars to any prospect who provides the appropriate information:

- "5 Tips for Parents on Navigating Financial Aid"
- "Career Planning for 20XX First-Years"
- "Online Learning: Is It Right for Me?"

- "Undeclared: What's Next for the Indecisive Student?"
- "Getting the Most out of the College Life"
- "Mastering Your Mental Health: Why It Matters to Students"
- "10 Tips and Tricks to Surviving Your First Year"

Always tailor content from your target audience's point of view and ask yourself, "Is this answering their questions?" Of course, brainstorming content is one thing. Getting it off the ground can be another matter altogether.

Here's my final tip! Check out the resources on our Tools page that can help provide clarity on your content marketing strategy. These are free and available at https://www.caylor-solutions.com/.

USE DISTINCTIVES IN LEAD GENERATION

Every educational institution, much like every individual, boasts its own distinctive fingerprint. The challenge often isn't the absence of uniqueness but the recognition of it.

Back in my grade school years, in a class of 20, we had three sets of twins. Three! For me, growing up immersed in that environment, this amount of twins felt entirely ordinary. It wasn't until I looked beyond the classroom walls that I realized how uncommon it actually was.

Institutions surrounded by their own everyday realities often fail to recognize their standout attributes.

They feel they are "just like" the other small institutions in their space. But even within identical twins, intricacies in personality, likes, dislikes, and quirks distinguish one from the other. And just as the twins could be distinguished from each other, so can institutions. No two institutions, no matter how alike in mission or curriculum, are carbon copies of each other. Look deeper, probe further, and bring into the limelight the aspects that set your institution apart. Harnessing this can significantly amplify your lead generation efforts.

Recently, on my podcast, Dr. Long, president of Saybrook University, identified some of the common marketing challenges all schools are facing in these unique modern times. The first challenge is a crisis of confidence in higher education from the general public. The second challenge is showing return on investment, especially now that students will likely have to take out numerous student loans. The third challenge we discussed was the general public's feeling that higher education institutions are overpriced.[53]

While these challenges do affect all schools in many ways, they impact small schools in particular. But even as a small school, you can highlight your brand distinctives through content storytelling in your marketing materials to stand out among the crowd.

If you can lean into what you offer, you can create a more integrated, individualized experience for those students seeking you out. Too many times, small schools tend to focus on what they don't have compared to others as opposed to what they do have. Instead, lean into your brand so you can show how your institution can benefit the life of your mission-fit student.

10

ADVANCEMENT MARKETING

For fundraising, major gifts, and donations, two terms are used interchangeably: "advancement" and "development." For this chapter, I've chosen to focus on advancement, but the difference between the two is important to note.

Advancement embodies a holistic strategy. At its core, it doesn't just aim for immediate fundraising gains, it also looks to cultivate a sustainable, lifelong bond with donors. Think of it as the effort to not just attract, but to also nurture and maintain lasting relationships with alumni, parents, and potential supporters. It weaves the narrative of the institution, celebrates its milestones, and conveys its visions for the future.

Development takes a more targeted stance with its crosshairs primarily set on fundraising. It pin-points immediate financial needs, be it for capital campaigns, scholarship drives, or specific institutional ventures. The messaging in development marketing is honed in on the tangible benefits of monetary contributions to particular projects.

Both play roles in the financial health of an institution, but the relationship-centric focus of advancement can often be more important for marketing teams to focus on. Development will likely end up under the umbrella of the advancement marketing and communications strategy.

We're zooming in on advancement because it focuses on the heart of what institutions truly need: long-term, meaningful relationships with their supporters. At the end of the lifecycle of a student, in a perfect world, they will eventually become a donor. And donors are often a major part of what keeps a school running.

For some schools, they might bring in about 10% of the money needed every year. For others, it's even more—sometimes as high as 100% of what's needed based on the mission! It's because of this that small schools and those with faith-based connections often lean on donors because the money they get from donations are a big part of their yearly budget. Every dollar helps the school run smoothly.

Which leaves higher-education marketing departments with a big job.

Not only are they trying to get students to enroll, but they also have to think about how to attract donors. Luckily, some of the tactics we have explained to find our mission-fit students and market to them can be reused.

DONOR FUNNEL

First, let's look at the donor funnel.

A student's journey doesn't end when they graduate. In many ways, it's just the beginning. The moment a student becomes an alum, the dynamic shifts, moving them from beneficiaries of the institution to potential benefactors. It's in this shift that many institutions unfortunately lose alums, especially if they only ask for money a few times a year and do nothing else to stay engaged with them.

The end of the enrollment funnel, where a student becomes an alumni, is the starting point for the donor funnel.

When we visualize these two funnels, we can't see them as two separate pathways. Instead, they are simply one road where one leads to the other. Each stage in the enrollment funnel sets the stage for the subsequent phases in the donor funnel.

What institutions need to understand is that this journey, especially the transition from being enrolled to becoming a donor, may not always be rapid. It could take years, sometimes even decades, for an alum to reach a position where they can contribute significantly.

But herein lies the magic: by viewing the funnels as a cohesive whole, schools can prepare for this extended strategy.

The foundation for this, just like with students, is built on relationships. You provide donors with opportunities, guiding them step by step, nurturing their connection to the institution until they transform into committed or major donors. And just as students need timely nudges or calls-to-action, so do potential donors. It's about making them see the bigger picture and the impact of their contributions.

The following is a list of the stages of the enrollment funnel, then the donor funnel together to present the life cycle of your prospective student. The goal of moving people along this path should be the goal of all your marketing efforts.

Enrollment Funnel:

1. Suspect: Someone who may not know about your school. Name recognition is the first step. Needs an introduction.

2. Prospective Student: Knows your name, but needs more information.

3. Informed Prospect: Knows more about the program (perhaps from a stealth search), but needs motivation to convert to next step.

4. Contacted Prospect: Relationship established at very basic level (may be automated through gated content) and has raised a hand to request more information.

5. Nurtured Prospect: Automated marketing has nurtured this prospect to provide deeper levels of information over time in order to develop into a warmer lead that will be taken over by a school representative.

6. Relationship: This prospect has established a relationship with a school representative. Still may be basic, but there is two-way communication human-to-human.

7. Visitor: Has visited campus for a tour or other event.

8. Basic Application: Has applied to the institution through form on website.

9. Completed Application: This prospect has completed ancillary elements required for consideration.

10. Accepted: Has been offered acceptance to the institution.

11. Deposited: Has made an initial deposit on the first-year tuition.

12. Registered: Has attended registration event to select classes and completed other necessary pre-enrollment elements.
13. Matriculated: Has shown up for classes and stayed beyond initial first few weeks.
14. Retained: Has completed first semester and enrolled in second semester of freshman year.
15. Retained Sophomore: Has completed first year, returned as second year student.
16. Retained Junior: Has completed first two years, returned as third year student.
17. Retained Senior+: Has completed first three years, returned as fourth year/fifth year student.
18. Graduate: Has completed necessary classwork to qualify for graduation.

Donor Funnel:
19. Alumni: Has entered into alumni status (goals may vary depending upon structure of alumni organization)
20. Donor-of-Record: Has made minimal donation as part of an annual giving or class gift to establish donor-of-record
21. Second-Time-Donor: Moved beyond donor of record to a second voluntary gift.
22. School Evangelist: Regularly recommends school to prospects and other donors.
23. Consistent Donor: Regular donor of the institution, often at minimal level but with consistency
24. Major Donor: Moved beyond consistency to larger gifts

25. Named Donor: Donating to larger projects with naming opportunities (may be as simple as family scholarship or faculty chair)
26. Planned Giving Donor: Has established provisions in will to benefit the school.

Looking at this list you might think this is way too much work for my marketing team to accomplish.

Here's the thing. When I talk to schools about their marketing goals, I find that they often have the same challenge: their goals are not nearly big enough. Don't stop with just the "Apply Now" button . . . that is only step 8 of the relationship life-cycle with a student. There is so much more to explore!

When planning out your marketing efforts, keep the larger picture top of mind: the success of both the student and the institution. That is where this list will help you most.

FINDING DONORS

At its core, fundraising, particularly for major gifts, is not one-size-fits-all. While many donors are alumni, a significant number come from varied backgrounds and affiliations, including church relations and corporate partnerships.

The heart of successful fundraising is a genuine human connection.

Instead of just approaching potential benefactors with a request for funds, fundraisers should present a well-thought-out proposal, underscoring the benefits for the donor. Consider the Bill and Melinda Gates Foundation, for example. They typically only give to causes that align closely with their passions. If a stranger knocked on their door and asked for money, without presenting a case for how it aligns with their passions, they would likely be turned away.

The key to understanding this dynamic is to know your donors as intimately as you know your students. Who are they? What do they want? What are their watering holes? And, what age are they?

Motivations to donate will differ across generations. Someone who attended school in the 1960s may have a completely different perspective than an alumnus from the 1980s. For instance, while a Baby Boomer might have profound nostalgia for their alma mater, a member of Gen Z might view their educational institution through a lens of networking opportunities or its impact on their career trajectory.

Simply put, a blanket marketing strategy for donors will not suffice. Fundraisers need to delve deep into persona, segmentation, understanding each donor's unique motivations, identities, and preferred methods of donation. While some may opt for straightforward cash donations, others might contribute through goods and services. Some donors wish for lasting legacies, choosing to recognize the school in their will, while others might seek immediate recognition, perhaps with their name gracing a new building. There are also donors who are driven by the desire to support students whose stories resonate with their own who focus on scholarship opportunities for the underprivileged.

Segmentation is an art. For instance, an end-of-year campaign might specifically target affinity groups, perhaps emphasizing STEM achievements to science graduates while focusing on artistic milestones for arts alumni. Another approach might involve segmentation based on graduation decades, using testimonials from notable alumni and recalling beloved faculty members from those years.

Both strategies will work, but only for specific people in your alumni list. Target donor wants, needs, and interests just like you do with your students. That's why storytelling is critical to the core of your school's donor-centric marketing strategy. Speaking to your donors' hearts is the first step to building a relationship that should pay dividends in your fundraising efforts.

DONOR-CENTRIC MARKETING

Your institution is not the hero of this story. The donor is.

Too often, I've seen schools shout from the rooftops how incredible they are and why they deserve philanthropic gestures while completely neglecting the donor's inclinations. A well-crafted donor-centric marketing strategy is critical to helping your institution build and, more importantly, retain donor relationships. That begins with making your donors the heroes of your school's story. But first, you have to find them.

Fundraising is about telling a story. Kenyon College exemplified this by weaving their donors into the narrative of their future. In 2021, they announced a staggering anonymous $100 million pledge for their institution. Kenyon weaved the story of that pledge around a shared objective to ensure other donors still felt valued and crucial to the school's future.

Janet Marsden, VP of Communications, Kenyon College, said, "[We had] alumni reflect on their own experience on campus and how this gift was going towards something that every alum could speak to [concerning] their experience on Kenyon's campus."[54]

Most donors aren't seeking fame or adoration. Instead, they're passionate about the cause and want to make a difference. Your donors won't simply give because you ask. You need to understand *why* they want to donate. To uncover this, partner with your marketing team to conduct research using these tools:

- Surveys
- Focus groups
- Social media polls
- Web traffic data

Once you understand where your donors want to see their donations go, ask yourself and your advancement team these questions before directly engaging with them:

- Does your school have a problem to solve?—Clearly define why you are appealing to your audience for a donation.
- What is your call to action?—Give your donor well-defined parameters on what (how much) they can give to help meet your goal.
- Does your case statement speak to your donor's emotions?—Be it concern, duty, or school pride, your fundraising appeal should evoke an emotional response.

By gaining a clear picture of what drives your donors to give, you can craft your donor-centric strategy so that their collective vision aligns with your own. Whether it's through a social media post or a letter in a mailbox, your advancement team needs to get personal in donor communications.

Want to build a much-needed extension for your athletic training facility? Reach out to former athletes with a personalized letter that recalls their days in your gym or on the field! Better yet, ask your coaches to send personalized videos to their old athletes, asking if they'd be willing to help the next generation of your school's competitors. Be it email, direct mail, social media, or other channels, you will significantly increase your donor engagement by tailoring personalized messaging to your intended audience.

No matter the situation, people like to feel appreciated. The same is true for your donors. Ensure your advancement team is putting in the effort to maintain regular contact with your school's donors and keeping them updated on relevant developments.

On a episode of our podcast, Amanda Nicol, Director Of Annual Giving at the University of Findlay, gave this advice on donor relationships: "When you are having a bad day, and all you hear is "no", call the best donor that you have and just have a conversation with them because they are the donor that is going to pick you up and make you feel good, and you're going to be able to have things to talk about, and it will turn your day around. And I will tell you that I have done that on more than one occasion. It is a hard place to be sometimes, and there are days and periods of time when you get a lot of nos and projects don't go the way you want them to. But there are those donors that are always a spotlight in your life."[55]

By engaging with your donors and building those enduring relationships, you'll create even more opportunities to invite them to expand on their philanthropic story. After all, they're the heroes, and they need to be acknowledged as such!

CAPITAL CAMPAIGNS

Few efforts get as much attention and institutional resources as capital campaigns. They require massive sustained effort over a long period of time.

It's not uncommon for these macro-campaigns to last anywhere from two to five years as institutions stretch themselves to raise large amounts of money for major campus renovations, new construction, financial aid, or endowment enhancement. To sustain this kind of long-term effort, institutions need buy-in from all departments, especially from the trustee board and executive teams. And marketing should be among the first teams to buy into the project.

A capital campaign is a focused effort by institutions to raise significant funds for specific goals, be it new buildings, scholarships, or other vital projects. This could be inclusive of:

- Building endowments
- Investing in infrastructure
- Establishing scholarships
- Funding faculty positions
- Augmenting the yearly budget

And these campaigns typically have three phases: feasibility study, planning phase, and the silent phase.

FEASIBILITY STUDY

A feasibility study involves bringing in experts to chat with alumni and major donors, gauging the level of support they can expect. It's like testing the waters before a big dive, ensuring they're not headed for a belly flop. And they typically outsource to a third party to help them with this phase.

This third party is usually external counsel, specialized in campaign feasibility studies, to gauge the potential for success. By liaising with alumni, major gift donors, and other stakeholders, these professionals aim to estimate the potential funds the institution can amass from its immediate network.

For marketers, this stage provides an opportunity to contribute by crafting a case statement—a document detailing the reasons for the campaign. This statement becomes an essential tool in understanding how receptive the donor base might be to the fundraising efforts.

PLANNING PHASE

Armed with insights from the feasibility study, the institution enters the planning phase. The focus here is on fine-tuning the campaign strategy based on the results of the feasibility study.

You might find donors didn't resonate with the first draft of your case statement or showed interest in other ways to donate. Take this information into consideration and align your capital campaign to their preferences. You'll have more success!

Here the previously drafted case statement is refined and finalized, serving as the backbone for all marketing materials and pitches within the campaign.

How To Craft a Winning Case Statement

The case statement is, in essence, the roadmap of a campaign, providing a transparent view into how donations are intended to be utilized. And, it's the blueprint that guides how funds will be used, segmented into different sectors based on the passions and motivations of potential donors.

For instance, the document might detail that a certain percentage of the collected funds will be directed towards the institution's endowment. Another portion could be allocated for shared professorships or scholarships. This segmentation isn't arbitrary. It's tailored to the varying passions of donors.

The challenge for marketers is to bring this financial roadmap to life. To craft a narrative that not only informs but tugs at the heartstrings, stirring emotion and illustrating why each allocation is not only necessary but transformative. It's about taking numbers and percentages and turning them into compelling stories that resonate, making potential donors not just understand, but feel the impact of their contribution.

Here are the 5 elements of an effective case statement:

1. Case Statement Element 1: Your Compelling Idea—The first element in creating a strong case for support is to craft your compelling idea. What is your vision statement? What are your value declarations?

2. Case Statement Element 2: Define the Problem—You need to show people the problems that your school solves through its educational programs. Whether it's a problem to solve or an opportunity to fulfill, it should be tied into that big compelling idea.

3. Case Statement Element 3: Show How You Solve the Problem—Describe how your school uniquely solves the problem you described earlier. This is probably the easiest step of all because you're describing your programs or the programs you're launching. Here we can describe our research project, our degree program, the new initiative, and the way we're partnering with the

community around community development or with the business sector around economic development.

4. Case Statement Element 4: Your Intended Results— Show your donor that the mission is, in fact, possible. Of course, that means that their charitable donation won't be in vain. One way we're going to do that is to measure for results. We're going to be able to describe to our donors that because of this program, something specific is going to happen.

5. Case Statement Element 5: Tailor Your Messaging— Customize your messaging to match the marketing channels we're using and the donors to whom we're reaching out to.

Finally, once the perfect case statement is crafted, it is often fielded to faculty and staff first. Not only is their contribution helpful, but if these core groups don't believe in the campaign's purpose, it is bound to face challenges. Their support serves as a testament to the campaign's worthiness.

SILENT & PUBLIC PHASES

When launching a capital campaign, many might assume that the real work begins once the campaign is announced publicly. However, by that time, a significant portion of the funds (often between 50-70%) has already been secured during the "Silent Phase."

These initial funds, often substantial, come from significant donors and form the bedrock of the campaign.

But this is where the challenge for marketers begins. They're tasked with raising the remaining 30% or so, which often comes from smaller donors. Specifically those who give between $10 and $15 each. Meeting this goal is crucial because some of the larger donors might hold back their pledges if the total goal isn't met. Thus, it's a race against time, where every donation, whether $5 or $10, becomes invaluable.

During the silent phase, and when the capital campaign goes public, consistent communication is pivotal. It's a good idea to explore online resources, like blog articles about capital campaigns, for inspiration. A dedicated section or microsite on an institution's main website can keep potential donors updated about the campaign's progress, often visualized with a progress bar, which gamifies the donation process and clearly shows everyone where you are in the fundraising efforts.

RELATIONSHIP IS EVERYTHING

As you tackle the ins and outs of fundraising and donor management, I urge you to remember one thing. At the very heart of it all is the essence of human connection—relationships.

When you peel back the layers of strategy, metrics, and campaigns, what you find is a network of intricate relationships guiding every action and decision.

Consider the role of an institution president. While they have numerous responsibilities, a significant part of their mandate is to raise funds. This isn't simply about approaching donors with a proposal; it's about leveraging the relationships they've nurtured over the years. As marketers, understanding the potential power of these relationships is pivotal. It means recognizing the influence wielded by not just the president, but board members, influential alumni, and other key stakeholders. Their stories, their testimonials, and their endorsements are invaluable tools in a marketer's arsenal, acting as catalysts for credibility and trust.

Why is this so effective? Because people are inherently drawn to personal stories and genuine relationships.

Donations are seldom made to faceless institutions. They are rooted in personal connections. Whether it's an alumnus wanting to honor a beloved professor with a scholarship or a community member wanting to support a student with potential, it's about the human stories intertwined with the institution. People are driven by their bonds, their memories, and their hopes for the future.

In the realm of higher education marketing, it's easy to get lost in the sea of tactics and lose sight of this foundational truth. But these relationships, whether with future peers, mentors, or professors, often become the determining factor in a student's decision to enroll and a donor's decision to give.

Another vital aspect is tracking donation records and ensuring timely, personal acknowledgment of every contribution. Personal touches matter. While a handwritten note from a student or president might sound old school, its power to foster connection is timeless. Keeping track of donation records and ensuring personal follow-ups and thank you gestures are all part of the charm. Especially when, in an age of technology the personal touch is a rare find.

An innovative tool like SpokeNote can marry the old and new. Imagine sending a postcard with a handwritten note combined with a QR code that plays a personalized video. It offers a donor the experience of reading your heartfelt gratitude while also seeing firsthand the difference their contribution made.

CREATE WAVES.
THINK DIFFERENTLY

Historically, institutions have shied away from viewing themselves through a commercial lens. Words like "sales" and "marketing" were whispered in hushed tones, if they were spoken at all. But times change, and any institution who still feels this way will get left behind.

Now, don't get me wrong. Many in the higher ed world are masters of their craft, adept at execution, and excellent predictors of trends. But where's the spark? The flair?

Every so often, someone strides into the higher ed scene with a fresh perspective—and it's often from fields you wouldn't expect. Like Anna-Maya Dalhgren who came from over a decade in service line marketing for one of the nation's leading health care systems with high ranking hospitals. When she made the switch from B2C healthcare marketing to higher education, she sought out my advice and coaching to fill in the gaps of what she needed to know. With her past experience, she came to higher education marketing with a fresh perspective, the willingness to try new ideas, and the ability she needed to apply best practices in higher ed marketing and build a team that could do the same.

Or take Brian Kenny of Harvard, who also came from a healthcare marketing background and stated on our podcast that higher ed was one of the toughest industries to market, and Jenny Petty from the University of Montana, who jumped in from the gaming industry with unique perspectives and exciting ideas. These higher ed marketing giants come from outside the higher ed realm and have drawn inspiration from several different industries.

Many people are good marketing *predictors*, meaning they are good at the craft and understand how to get things done. But they have a lack of imagination and creativity to generate new ideas. This could be due to the tradition of academia, or it could be because there are not as many entrepreneurial spirits within higher ed. But when you are lacking ideas, you can always steal like an artist.

Great artists "steal"—they borrow and reshape from what they see around them. When artists "steal" they aren't copying someone else, they are inspired by someone else and reshaping the thing that inspired them. Just like when one song sounds like another! Austin Kloen's book "Steal Like An Artist"[56] talks about this concept often.

For example, "Uptown Funk" by Bruno Mars and Mark Ronson has been influenced by multiple existing songs, contributing to its widespread popularity. According to WhoSampled, the song incorporates at least five known different samples—the practice of taking a portion of a sound recording and reusing it in a different song.[57] But according to Wikipedia, it could be more.[58] The familiarity of these samples and influences likely plays a part in why the song resonates with so many people. It melds elements from both past and present into a harmonious whole.

You can borrow what's successful for others too. That doesn't mean you copy it outright. It means when something is working, you try to figure out *why* it is working, then re-engineer the concept for your own needs. It's about catching the essence, not replicating every brush stroke.

Northern Higher University (NHU) is often seen as a marketing juggernaut of higher ed because they've mastered the art of making the student the centerpiece and hero of their marketing. They don't just say, "Earn a degree"; they scream, "Transform your life!" It's not about the journey, but the life-altering change post-degree. This works because people don't want to buy a degree, they want to buy the outcome of what life will be after the degree. Show the outcome.

Too many small schools give me the excuse that they simply "can't compete" with the big schools. But when I dig into their marketing strategy, I usually find it's not that they can't compete, it's that they are trying to duplicate what the big institutions do. Which small institutions simply can't duplicate.

Remember, you need to find *your* mission-fit student and market to them.

DISCOMFORT IS GOOD

Have you ever felt hesitation or worry when you try something new? Believe it or not, this is actually a positive sign. Feeling a bit uneasy or uncomfortable can be a catalyst for creativity when you're deep in the process of using your imagination. It pushes you out of your comfort zone, challenging you to think in new ways and come up with innovative solutions you might not have considered otherwise.

Instead of sticking to your safe bubble, get curious. Take a peek into other industries or even the hobbies you adore. You might be surprised how a tech solution could inspire a brilliant educational campaign, or how your love for baking gives a fresh spin on student engagement. When looking for inspiration you'll likely find that "Aha!" moment in unexpected places.

And remember you aren't alone! You can brainstorm with others, or you could even throw the concept into ChatGPT and ask AI to brainstorm a concept with you. I also find asking AI to explain a concept like I'm a five-year-old or to provide analogies that simplify what I'm trying to say helps to see things from a different angle.

Just remember, it's the tiny grain of sand that irritates the oyster, which then produces a pearl. But without that gain of sand to irritate the oyster, the pearl would never exist. Similarly, introducing that irritation or discomfort into your creative process can create pearls you hadn't thought of before. Pearls of wisdom, if you will.

Sometimes people get concerned that if they push the envelope on creativity, they will offend those they are trying to attract, or those they report to will say the campaign is not academic or serious enough. I've even heard this when I try to push the envelope. But I am also quick to remind them that it isn't about what they think, it's about what the mission-fit student thinks. If you know the prospective student and what appeals to them, and if you can get them excited about being a part of your institution, you need to trust your gut, confirm through informal focus groups with current students, and go with that.

While some may worry that bold creativity could offend potential students or higher-ups, it's essential to focus on what truly resonates with your mission-fit students. I was reminded of this during a podcast conversation with Mary Barr, Chief Marketing Officer at Ball State University.[59] Mary shared a simple yet highly effective strategy she uses every year. During orientation, she sits down with a handful of new students to casually discuss what brought them to the institution. She asks them about the marketing messages that struck a chord and what ultimately compelled them to choose the school. This interaction, although informal, is a goldmine of information that aids in refining marketing approaches.

The conventional approach of hiring external agencies to conduct formal focus groups often seems like the "safe" route but can overlook the immediate, candid feedback that students are willing to share. These casual conversations offer an authentic snapshot of what influenced their decision-making process, and because she repeats this exercise annually, she can make continual adjustments to her marketing strategy.

This should serve as a lesson for higher education leaders and Chief Marketing Officers (CMOs). Instead of relying solely on formal methods, seize the available opportunities to directly interact with your new student population. Not only is this a cost-effective approach, but it can also give you an immediate pulse on what's working and what's not. Trust your instincts and corroborate your strategies with new students at your institution. It might be uncomfortable at first, but it is highly effective.

Joanne Soliday, the author of "Pivot: A Vision For The New University," wrote, "The fundamental predicate for a culture of risk-taking and innovation is that experimentation is essential to discovering better ways of doing things with speed and flexibility, especially in this world of rapid change and adaptation."[60]

And I believe she's right. The world's changing fast. She goes on to say, "... courageous leaders put a laser focus on: ... breaking down the barriers to innovation and risk-taking within the culture and organization of the faculty. Abandoning the notion of consensus in favor of adaptation; action ..."

Higher education is no stranger to the transformative forces of change. From artificial intelligence to looming enrollment cliffs and mounting financial pressures, the challenges are numerous and complex. Unfortunately, higher education tends to be risk-averse, an attitude that exacerbates these issues. There's a tipping point where the onslaught of change becomes too much to handle, especially if institutions are not open to innovative solutions.

For higher education marketing leaders and Chief Marketing Officers, the ability to innovate should not just be a talking point—it needs to be a foundational strategy. Open conversations among cabinet members about taking calculated risks and experimenting with new approaches can serve as an early indicator of an institution's future success or failure.

Avoiding conversations about risk-taking and innovation can result in reactive decision-making, which is rarely in the institution's best interest. When change is ignored, it doesn't disappear; it simply accumulates until the institution is *forced* to change. Which culminates in last-minute decisions when the pressure becomes too great to ignore.

In these instances, there is little time for the thoughtful evaluation and experimentation that could identify the most effective strategies for adaptation. Instead, leaders are forced into a corner where they must make quick, sometimes ill-considered choices just to keep the wheels turning. This reactive approach not only increases the likelihood of errors but also misses the opportunity for groundbreaking improvements that a more proactive, experimental mindset could offer.

Sticking to what's safe and familiar isn't going to change anything. It's comfortable, sure, but it's also boring. If you're brave and you take those leaps of faith, that's when things shift to eye-catching marketing. In today's competitive education landscape, standing out matters.

LOOK OUTSIDE THE NORM

Don't fall into the trap of thinking you sell the same thing as every other school.

Recently, I listened to an audiobook called *Unreasonable Hospitality* by Will Guidara, and I loved the concepts discussed within.[61] The book is written by a restaurant owner and his chef who took on the restaurant together. Under their management, the restaurant went from a two-Michelin-star restaurant to a four-Michelin-star restaurant.

How? Unreasonable hospitality.

They did things that changed the way people felt. In this restaurant, every time a patron came in, they would ask how they got here, and if the patron drove and parked on the street. If they did, the restaurant staff would ask what their car looked like, where it was parked, then take care of the meter while they were in the restaurant so they wouldn't have to worry about it. And their coat check is amazing as well. The staff didn't give patrons a tag for coat check. Instead, they tagged the coats with a table number. When that table stood up to leave, the coat check was sure to have their coats ready and waiting for them by the time they got to the door.

Another couple celebrating their anniversary mentioned to their waiter that they had a bottle of champagne waiting for them in the freezer. They had never done this before, and asked the waiter if the champagne would be okay. The waiter informed them it would likely explode, then asked for their keys, went to their apartment, and moved it from the freezer to the fridge. But he didn't stop there—he also left chocolate and flowers on the counter! Crazy right? How would you feel if someone did this for you?

With unreasonable hospitality, they turned the restaurant into an *experience*.

If restaurant owners can do this, you can too during your campus tour. Think about the impression you would leave on potential students if you treated them with unreasonable hospitality. If you can take something that is expected and make it into the unbelievable, you will quickly gain loyal followers. The companies and brands that stand out are going above and beyond what people expect. The best part is that many times, doing the unexpected doesn't cost any extra money.

You can also make an impression before anyone even steps foot on your campus. Remember when I brought up Butler Blue in Chapter 7, and the unique postcards the campus bulldog would send? Butler University did this for my son before he ever stepped foot on their campus. You see, they used their living mascot Blue, a 65-pound English bulldog to reach out to prospective students. He has also become the voice of the school on their social media pages.

As a Bulldog, Blue can say cute—and sometimes cheeky—things on his social media to lighten up the Butler brand without causing any harm. He makes their platform fun and unique.

And then Butler began sending Butler Blue on admissions visits for some high-touch marketing. Now he often surprises students with their letter of admission right on their doorstep! With the help of Blue IV, Butler's admissions team has delivered almost 400 offers of admission over the last five to six years. In these past years, the Butler Bulldog has surprised prospective students at homes, schools, and even gained a substantial social media following.

I'd say Blue is a reason my son, Ben, is now a Butler graduate. Butler University was one of many schools my son applied to around the nation, and even after receiving his acceptance letters (from Butler and others), he still hadn't decided which institution was right for him. But, one Saturday, we found two letters from Butler University on the counter that changed the game. One was addressed to Tigger, our dog, and the other was addressed to Stormy, our cat.

Inside the letter to Tigger, Blue "wrote" a dog-to-dog type of conversation. He congratulated Tigger for his human being accepted to Butler University and promised he was going to protect Ben just as if he were his very own human, proceeding with more details of next steps.

For the cat, it was a little bit more tepid. Basically, it started with "Hey, your human has been accepted. But I know I'm a dog and you're a cat. Let's respect each other . . ."

It was brilliant copywriting! My son was thrilled that the marketing team at Butler had taken the time to tailor their communication in such a personal way through Blue. They entered a part of his world that no one else had, and it worked.

Guess where my son decided to go?

STAND OUT TO SURVIVE

Remember, innovation isn't just about newness—it's about value.

Small institutions, more than their expansive counterparts, are in a unique position to harness the power of distinction. They have the agility to change, pivot, and reinvent comes easier to those who aren't weighed down by bureaucratic processes or layers of traditionalism.

And by re-positioning your school's offering, you can resonate deeply with your mission-fit students, the ones who will thrive in your ecosystem. It's about understanding a student's hopes, dreams, fears, and aspirations—then reflecting those understandings in every interaction, every campaign, and every course.

Remember, if your institution can be the place where a student feels seen, heard, and valued, you've already won half the battle.

YOU CAN DO THIS.
HERE'S A ROADMAP

Every institution, big or small, has a unique value, story, and brand. I've worked with small institutions who only have a handful of students, to giants like Western Governors University with enrollments of 100,000. Whether big or small, I've always found they have something different to offer from the others. Each one has distinct cultures, histories, strengths, and challenges.

Each one has the potential to utilize the marketing tactics I have outlined. With the right roadmap, you can effectively market your institution. Don't get me wrong—it takes hard work. But if you embrace courage and your creative side, you'll be surprised to see what you can do. No ifs, ands, or buts. It doesn't matter if your budget doesn't rival the largest of endowments. It's not about the glossy brochures or the star-studded list of alumni.

It is about setting your institution apart, identifying your mission-fit student, and speaking to them at their watering holes. So, the next time that tiny voice of doubt whispers, suggesting you don't have the right money, resources, or knowledge to excel . . . silence it.

YOU CAN DO THIS

We're at the tail end of our journey together, and if there's one thing I want to echo loud and clear, it's this: *You can absolutely do this.*

Throughout these pages, I've handed you tools, strategies, and insights, so you can help your institution speak to the mission-fit students who need you. Because not only does your institution deserve to thrive, but the students who need you deserve to find you. And that won't happen unless you are speaking directly to them.

I believe in the power and good that higher education can bring into someone's life. I want to help you help students thrive. You see, I'm a first-gen student. In high school, the idea of higher education seemed as distant as the moon. Not because I didn't want to reach out and touch it, but because I genuinely didn't know how. Additional schooling wasn't a dinner table discussion in my household, and no one in my family before me had walked that path.

Fast-forward to today—I can say my education experience changed the course of my life. It has taken me places I didn't expect. It was an investment in the future of my family. Every lecture, every paper, every interaction opened up opportunities for me, my wife (another first-generation student) and ultimately our four children. My education was an investment, one that continually pays me back to this day.

Even though through my career I have worked with some of the world's largest consumer brands, I choose to dedicate the second half of my career working exclusively with higher ed institutions because of this experience. I want each institution to attract the mission-fit student who will thrive at their campus, just as I did at my alma mater. This book is filled with the ideas, insights, and strategies I've gained by dedicating my career to helping higher education institutions better market themselves. While I can't say it's not hard work, I can say this book is the cheat code you need to find success in the journey.

But if ever you feel overwhelmed or find yourself at a crossroads, remember you're not alone. Whether it's through my podcasts, blog articles, ebooks, or consulting, I'm here to guide and support you. Your potential is boundless, and I wholeheartedly believe in your capacity to make waves in the world of higher education.

MAKE SURE ADMINISTRATION HAS YOUR BACK

From my point of view, the main point of marketing at any institution is to support and enhance net revenue-focused efforts by prioritizing the most profitable channel, which is enrollment.

Far too often, higher education marketers have become "short order cooks" taking orders and flipping them in a "first-in-first-out" mentality. No more letting internal campus teams call the shots on what marketing "needs" to do. The marketing team needs to be the "chefs" who are highly focused on enrollment strategy. If someone needs a quick brochure or event flier, they can outsource that work with a clearly defined brand guidebook.

I can't stress this enough—without the president having your back, it's like trying to steer a ship without a compass. They need to stand tall and send a clear message to the faculty and everyone else: *Marketing isn't just a support function to be summoned randomly. It is a mission-critical department meant to identify, enhance, and sustain enrollment efforts.*

REMEMBER YOUR ROADMAP

Throughout this book I've walked you through this plan, but we'll review it concisely here.

Start by identifying your mission-fit student.

This is your cornerstone. It's the foundation on which every other brick of your marketing strategy will lay. Now, I understand. Maybe you're wrestling with your institution's brand identity. Maybe words escape you when you try to articulate what makes your institution unique. But remember, within the walls of your institution, there are stories of success. Students who have not only thrived on your campus but are also flourishing in their respective fields.

Dive deep into these success stories. Understand the traits that allowed these students to shine. What made them resonate with your institution's ethos? These students, their characteristics, their passions, their aspirations, they embody what you're looking for—they are your mission-fit students.

Understanding who they are is the starting point from which you can engineer your strategy. Once you pinpoint this, the rest follows.

Then, find the watering holes for your mission-fit students.

Just like a watering hole in the African Savanna, in the digital and real world, there are specific spots where your mission-fit students gather. These are their "watering holes," and it's essential to pinpoint them.

It might be tempting to cast a wide net, hoping to attract all sorts of students. But that's a mistake! The real trick is in the precision of your efforts. Maybe your mission-fit student is an Instagram aficionado, posting stories about their academic achievements. Or perhaps they're engrossed in their local church community or spending weekends at neighborhood coffee shops. Each student's journey is unique, and their preferred spots will vary. Rather than spreading yourself thin, dive deep into these niches. Tailor your marketing strategies to where they are most likely to be seen, and you'll see a more genuine, engaged response.

It's about quality, not quantity!

Next, harness your unique edge.

What makes your school stand out? It's not just about the courses you offer or the facilities you have, but the singular experiences, values, and narratives unique to your institution.

Start by taking a holistic view of your school. Beyond the academic achievements and facilities, delve into the stories that have shaped the institution. Are there traditions, success stories, or even challenges-turned-opportunities that define your journey? These nuances often resonate deeper than generic statistics.

Next, tailor these unique traits to speak directly to your mission-fit student. For instance, if your institution has a strong culture of community service and you've identified that your mission-fit students value giving back, spotlight stories of student-led initiatives, community impacts, or faculty projects would be a good way to capture their attention. Or, maybe there is a unique mentorship program or a distinct approach to experiential learning at your institution. Ask yourself how this might align with what your mission-fit students seek within their academic journey.

Your uniqueness is not just about being different—it's about being *relevant*.

Next, create content that resonates with these students.

Once you've identified who your mission-fit students are and where they hang out, the next piece of the puzzle is delivering content that captivates. It's not about creating content for the sake of content. It's about creating narratives, stories, and information that resonate with these specific students, answering their questions, easing their concerns, and igniting their interest.

Start by gathering intelligence from the frontlines. Who better to provide insights than your admissions team? They're the ones fielding queries, addressing concerns, and guiding prospects daily. Organize a brainstorming session with them and curate a list of the top 50 questions that prospective students frequently pose. These questions reveal the pressing concerns, aspirations, and curiosities of those considering joining your institution.

From here, the task is straightforward: Answer these questions, but do so with the mission-fit student in mind. Don't forget the importance of an enrollment-focused website. Having highly relevant content with an enrollment-focused website is a slam dunk in terms of attracting your mission-fit student. Doing one without the other is a missed opportunity.

Next, identify your top 5-7 high-demand programs.

These programs are likely the reason your mission-fit students will consider your institution. If you don't know what they are, chat with your deans or institutional effectiveness office (this is the group that submits the yearly data reports for accreditation).

Every program at your institution is awesome in its own right, but you can't give them all the spotlight. This isn't meant to undermine the value of other programs; it's simply a matter of strategic focus. Some folks might not be thrilled with this approach, but keep your eye on the prize. The goal is to get more students through those doors who will resonate with these eye-catching programs.

Once they're hooked, they'll naturally explore all the other cool stuff your school offers.

Finally, put the plan together and stick to it.

All right, you have done the groundwork. Now, it's time to connect the dots and roll out the big game plan. Gone are the days of being short order cooks! Now you are a strategist whose number one priority is to boost enrollment numbers.

Now that you know who your mission-fit students are, understand where they gather, and what they want to know, you have to execute. With a plan in hand, it's all about staying the course. If you've got clarity on where to market, what makes you special, and you're armed with content that hits home, half the battle's won. All that's left? Stick to the lead generation tactics in Chapter 9 and watch the magic unfold.

Remember, your mission-fit students aren't just wandering around aimlessly. They're searching for you, ready to call your institution home. Help them see you loud and clear in their preferred watering holes, and show them why you are the best institution for them.

Get out there and chase your mission-fit student!

CONCLUSION

As we draw to a close, I'm overwhelmed with gratitude. Writing this book has been a journey of passion, experience, and a deep desire to make a difference in the realm of higher education marketing. And for you, the reader, to invest your time and trust in these pages is an honor I don't take lightly. Your dedication to chasing mission-fit students who will succeed at your institution showcases your commitment.

And it all starts with the pivotal question: *Why should a student pick your school?*

Your mission-fit students are out there, searching for an institution that genuinely fills them up and makes them feel connected. The magic lies in understanding what you have to offer, positioning your institution as the undeniable answer, and removing the friction it takes to become a student on your campus.

We have talked about the challenges faced by marketing professionals in the education sector. From restrictive budgets to the misconceptions about marketing's role, it often feels like a battle. But marketing is not about grand budgets or vast teams.

Instead, marketing is about clearly defining and communicating your unique proposition so you can create revenue generating opportunities for your institution. Without this clarity, your message becomes just another voice amidst the clamor, fading into the background.

My connection to education as a first-generation student has only intensified my belief in its power. This book, stemming from my heart and a synthesis of my years in marketing, has been my way of helping you—the gatekeepers of these institutions—find your voices and ensure that the right students find their way to you.

The success stories from Caylor Solutions are a testament to the fact that every institution has a compelling story, waiting to be told. Your niche positioning, even if yet undiscovered, can be the launchpad for compelling, audience-focused marketing. This book arms you with the strategies and insights to tap into that potential.

Thank you for joining me on this journey. If you ever find yourself needing more guidance or insights, remember, I have several resources available to you. From my podcast to online masterclasses and virtual conferences, I'm here to support you every step of the way. Just go to https://thehigheredmarketer.com/ for more insights. You can also partner with us directly to get creative and customized solutions for education marketing at https://www.caylor-solutions.com/.

Here's to charting new paths, finding mission-fit students, and transforming lives. Remember, you've got this, and I'm right here cheering you on!

ACKNOWLEDGMENTS

I have dreamt of writing a book for many years. But you know what? It's a lot of work! And in all fairness, I hadn't clearly defined what I wanted to share. However, during these last few years, I have had the opportunity to more fully articulate the deepest passions that drive me: my gratitude for how higher education impacted my life and that of my family; how much opportunity there is for higher education through the right kind of marketing and communication; and the passion and fulfillment that drives me to partner with others to help them achieve their very best.

Having such passions only comes up short without the support of the people God has brought into my life to encourage and assist me in seeing this book come to fruition. First, I am grateful for my wife, Dana, and her consistent support and partnership in all my life. Her encouragement and gentle challenges throughout my life have led me to where I am today. I also appreciate my children, Ben, Nathan, Ash, and Lily, for their consistent support and trust.

I also want to recognize those who have helped make me a better person. Part of that started early with my parents, who encouraged me, and my siblings, who challenged me. Thanks, Mom and Dad, Jeff, and Julie.

I was also blessed to have teachers along the way that made learning fun, like my third-grade teacher Betty Kanuas and my high school German teacher, Karen Claypool. And along the way during my career, mentors and business partners like Rob Kearns, Ed Illig, Bob Blass, and Jim Wolfe helped me grow in my craft; influencers such as Mike Collete, Steve Mortland, Jeff Bergerren, Roger Kieffer, and Dan Sanchez challenged me in my efforts. Partners in work such as Tim Fuller, Dave Burke, Phil Cook, David Medders, Philip Dearborn, Carol Dibble, Troy Singer, and Robb Conolon have made it a joy to serve in what I believe God has called me to. I am also grateful for cheerleaders such as Chris Ropozo, Brad Entwhisle, Adam Metcalf, Soup Harrison, Raffi Der Simonian, Brian Jones, David Mezera, Dena Cambra, and a host of others who regularly provide encouragement and direction.

My team at Caylor Solutions and The Higher Ed Marketer have also played a huge role in giving me the room and encouragement to create this book. That includes our core members, such as Beth Mills, Jennifer Johnfauno, Jessi Robbins, Zach and Becca Coffin, Dustin and Hannah Wilson, Jen Munsel, Danielle Swyers, Faith Davila, Holly Smith, Sheila Addison, Matt Bloom, Jenni Roberts, Tim Altman, John McKinney, and Stephanie Griesch. I am also extremely grateful to Danielle Harward for helping me get all of this out of my head and into a comprehensive book.

It is also worth mentioning the numerous client interactions and podcast guests that I regularly learn from. You all have taught me and provided exceptional insights. Your fingerprints are on this book.

Thank you to each and every one of you. This book wouldn't be a reality without your influence in my life.

NOTES

INTRODUCTION
1. Caylor, B. & Singer, T. (2023, June 30). I Want to See the Dorm Room: Marketing Insights From Guy Kawasaki [Audio podcast episode]. *The Higher Ed Marketer*. https://www.higheredmarketerpodcast.com/i-want-to-see-the-dorm-room-marketing-insights-from-guy-kawasaki/
2. Team CSG. (2023, January 18). From https://wearecsg.com/blog/advertising-in-higher-education/

CHAPTER 1
3. Bransberger, P., Falkenstern, C., & Lane, P. (2020). From Knocking at the College Door: https://knocking.wiche.edu/data/knocking-10th-data/
4. Mayorga, N. (2021, August 26). From https://www.jamesgmartin.center/2021/08/did-you-know-college-closures-and-mergers-since-2016/

5. Toness, B. V., & Lurye, S. (2023, February 9). From https://projects.apnews.com/features/2023/missing-children/index.html
6. Kline, M. (2019). From https://www.cupahr.org/issue/feature/higher-ed-enrollment-cliff/
7. Bransberger, P., Falkenstern, C., & Lane, P. (2020). From Knocking at the College Door: https://knocking.wiche.edu/data/knocking-10th-data/
8. Harris, R. (2023, October 16). From https://nutmegeducation.com/how-many-colleges-are-in-the-us
9. Caylor, B. & Singer, T. (2021, June 29). Proven Strategies to Help the Next Generation Thrive w/ Mark McCrindle [Audio podcast episode]. *The Higher Ed Marketer*. https://www.higheredmarketerpodcast.com/proven-strategies-to-help-the-next-generation-thrive-w-mark-mccrindle/
10. McCrindle, M. (2023). *Generation Alpha*.
11. (2020, January 16). From Big 3 Media: https://www.big3.sg/blog/capturing-gen-zs-attention-the-most-important-8-seconds
12. Baer, J. (2013). *YoUtility:*.
13. Nietzel, M. T. (2022, May 11). From https://www.forbes.com/sites/michaeltnietzel/2022/05/11/more-than-39-million-americans-have-attended-college-but-earned-no-degree/?sh=7808d1713cd3

CHAPTER 2

14. Caylor, B. & Singer, (2022, October 11). Video QR Codes: Sticky Notes for the TikTok Generation [Audio podcast episode]. *The Higher Ed Marketer*. https://www.

higheredmarketerpodcast.com/video-qr-codes-sticky-notes-for-the-tiktok-generation/

15. Red Bull. (2017, November 28). *2 Wingsuit Flyers BASE Jump Into a Plane In Mid-Air | A Door In The Sky.* [Video]. YouTube. https://www.youtube.com/watch?v=YL9sNrOlK-I

16. Red Bull. (2012, October 14). *Felix Baumgartner's supersonic freefall from 128k' - Mission Highlights.* [Video]. YouTube. https://youtu.be/FHtvDA0W34I?si=2wDtAT3d5sVLP0-D

17. Liquid Death. (2023). *Greatest Hates, Vol. 3.* [Audio]. Spotify. https://open.spotify.com/album/2ml RoR7OFIJWiYf30M4OnY?si=RrX6m AwxSf2q1S3cD9jX7Q

18. (2023). From Kickstarter: https://www.kickstarter.com/projects/joinflashback/flashback-a-camera-for-the-small-moments

19. Deaton, J. P. (n.d.). From https://auto.howstuffworks.com/why-the-ford-edsel-failed.htm

CHAPTER 3

20. Caylor, B. & Singer, T. (2023, June 20). I Want to See the Dorm Room: Marketing Insights From Guy Kawasaki [Audio podcast episode]. *The Higher Ed Marketer.* https://www.higheredmarketerpodcast.com/i-want-to-see-the-dorm-room-marketing-insights-from-guy-kawasaki/

21. Buchholz, K. (2023, July 7). From https://www.statista.com/chart/29174/time-to-one-million-users/#:~:text=When%20Netflix%20was%20launched%20as,back%20then%2C%20movie%20mailorder%20

service.&text=This%20chart%20shows%20the%20
time,to%20reach%20one%20million%20users

22. Patel, N. (n.d.). From https://neilpatel.com/blog/38-content-marketing-stats-that-every-marketer-needs-to-know/#:~:text=Conversion%20rates%20are%20nearly%20
6x,rates%20by%20more%20than%205x

23. Canva. (n.d.). https://www.canva.com/for-campus/

24. (n.d.). From Oscar Mayer: https://www.oscarmayer.com/wienermobile

25. Toffler, A. (1970). Future Shock.

26. Yes, I do understand David was also blessed by God, and that blessing is largely responsible for his success. But this story still illustrates my point that many times we work in harmony with greater purposes by being thoughtful and strategic. Check out the full story in 1 Samuel 17.

CHAPTER 4

27. Caylor, B. & Singer, T. (2022, March 8). Confronting the "H-Bomb": The Truth About Managing a Popular Brand [Audio podcast episode]. *The Higher Ed Marketer*. https://www.higheredmarketerpodcast.com/confronting-the-h-bomb-the-truth-about-managing-a-popular-brand/

CHAPTER 5

28. Many people attribute this quote to Einstein, but this is a common misconception. In reality, the phrase appears in the 1983 novel "Sudden Death" by Rita Mae Brown. Although its origins can be traced back to at least the 19th century, there's no definitive evidence linking it to any historical figure like Einstein. https://www.history.com/news/here-are-6-things-albert-einstein-never-said

29. Caylor, B. & Singer, T. (2022, December 6). Easy to Apply, Hard to Ask: Addressing Your School Website's Focus [Audio podcast episode]. *The Higher Ed Marketer*. https://www.higheredmarketerpodcast.com/easy-to-apply-hard-to-ask-addressing-your-school-websites-focus/

CHAPTER 6

30. Varhatiuk, K. (2023, June 29). From https://fireart.studio/blog/modern-website-design-trends-with-examples-and-tips-for-designing-a-website
31. Caylor, B. & Singer, T. (2022, December 6). Easy to Apply, Hard to Ask: Addressing Your School Website's Focus [Audio podcast episode]. *The Higher Ed Marketer*. https://www.higheredmarketerpodcast.com/easy-to-apply-hard-to-ask-addressing-your-school-websites-focus/
32. Howarth, J. (2023, November 1). From https://explodingtopics.com/blog/mobile-internet-traffic
33. If you don't already filter your statistics, be sure to set one up so you can better measure the success of your campaigns for external audiences.
34. (n.d.). From LinkedIn: https://www.linkedin.com/pulse/learn-how-exclude-internal-traffic-ga4-like-pro/

CHAPTER 7

35. Weiners, P. (2017, July 24). From https://www.forbes.com/sites/forbescommunicationscouncil/2017/07/24/what-we-talk-about-when-we-talk-about-brand-authority/?sh=3cc6b94c5621
36. Maxwell, J. (n.d.). From https://www.goodreads.com/quotes/479285-he-who-thinks-he-leads-but-has-no-followers-is

37. Caylor, B. (2014, July 3). From Caylor Solutions: https://www.caylor-solutions.com/data-web-social-media-for-higher-education/
38. Pulizzi, J. (2023). Epic Content Marketing.
39. Caylor, B. (2023, June 26). From Caylor Solutions: https://www.caylor-solutions.com/proactive-content-marketing-strategy/
40. If you would like to see this postcard, check it out at: www.caylor-solutions.com/how-a-postcard-from-1952-can-help-you-get-started-in-content-marketing/
41. Baer, J. (2013). YoUtility:.
42. (n.d.). From Optin Monster: https://optinmonster.com/social-proof-statistics/#:~:text=70%25%20of%20people%20will%20trust,business's%20star%20rating%20is%20accurate
43. Funk, M. (2020, February 7). From https://www.tubics.com/blog/youtube-2nd-biggest-search-engine
44. Vogels, E. A., Gelles-Watnick, R., & Massarat, N. (2022, August 10). From https://www.pewresearch.org/internet/2022/08/10/teens-social-media-and-technology-2022/

CHAPTER 8

45. (n.d.). From American Marketing Association: https://www.ama.org/the-definition-of-marketing-what-is-marketing/#:~:text=Content%20Marketing,of%20driving%20profitable%20customer%20action
46. Caylor, B. & Singer, T. (2023, August 8). Content Marketing: Its Strengths, Weaknesses, And Everything In Between [Audio podcast episode]. *The Higher Ed Marketer*. https://

www.higheredmarketerpodcast.com/content-marketing-its-strengths-weaknesses-and-everything-in-between/

47. Suess, J. (2017, October 4). From https://www.cincinnati.com/story/news/2017/10/04/our-history-p-g-put-soap-soap-opera/732149001/

48. Caylor, B. & Singer, T. (2023, May 9). Seek the Unexpected: Surprising Students With Real Storytelling [Audio podcast episode]. *The Higher Ed Marketer.* https://www.higheredmarketerpodcast.com/seek-the-unexpected-surprising-students-with-real-storytelling/

49. Google now uses continuous scroll, so there is technically no longer a page two . . . but bodies can still be buried below the scroll.

50. Funk, M. (2020, February 7). From https://www.tubics.com/blog/youtube-2nd-biggest-search-engine

51. Dorney, H. (n.d.). From https://business.twitter.com/en/blog/how-to-create-and-use-hashtags.html#:~:text=On%20Twitter%2C%20adding%20a%20%E2%80%9C%23,that%20they're%20interested%20in

52. Kirkpatrick, M. (2011, February 4). From https://readwrite.com/the_first_hashtag_ever_tweeted_on_twitter_-_they_s/

CHAPTER 9

53. Caylor, B. & Singer, T. (2022, November 1). How to Articulate Distinctiveness: Making Your Small School Stand Out [Audio podcast episode]. *The Higher Ed Marketer.* https://www.higheredmarketerpodcast.com/how-to-articulate-distinctiveness-making-your-small-school-stand-out/

54. Caylor, B. & Singer, T. (2021, May 11). Campus Campaigns That Work: How to Include Donor Stories in Your Marketing [Audio podcast episode]. *The Higher Ed Marketer*. https://www.higheredmarketerpodcast.com/campus-campaigns-that-work-how-to-include-donor-stories-in-your-marketing/

55. Caylor, B. & Singer, T. (2023, January 10). Pay It Forward: Higher Ed Advancement and Philanthropy [Audio podcast episode]. *The Higher Ed Marketer*. https://www.higheredmarketerpodcast.com/pay-it-forward-higher-ed-advancement-and-philanthropy/

CHAPTER 10

56. Kleon, A. (2012). Steal Like an Artist.

57. (n.d.). From WhoSampled: https://www.whosampled.com/Uptown-Funk-Empire/

58. (n.d.). From Wikipedia: https://en.wikipedia.org/wiki/Uptown_Funk

59. Caylor, B. & Singer, T. (2021, July 6). Transition, Reaction, & Tapping Student Expertise w/ Mary Barr [Audio podcast episode]. *The Higher Ed Marketer*. https://www.higheredmarketerpodcast.com/transition-reaction-tapping-student-expertise-w-mary-barr/

CHAPTER 11

60. Soliday, J. (2019). Pivot: A Vision For The New University.

61. Guidara, W. (2022). Unreasonable Hospitality.

ABOUT THE AUTHOR

62. I started my career in 1987 when I was a senior in high school doing design and marketing for AU's dining service. With that math, I am coming up on 40 years in 2027.

ABOUT THE AUTHOR

With a career spanning over 35 years,[62] Bart Caylor has leveraged a vast experience which he utilizes for his clients. As a partner at one of Indianapolis's largest digital design and branding firms, Bart directed and consulted with a number of higher education accounts throughout his 14 year tenure. He was also the driving force behind new media initiatives for clients such as Motorola, Ingersoll Rand, Roche Diagnostics, Community Health Network, RCA, Schlage Lock, and Lexmark.

Bart now leads Caylor Solutions and The Higher Ed Marketer, applying his marketing knowledge and skills specifically to the education industry. His work has garnered acclaim in *The Chronicle of Higher Education*, *How Magazine*, and *U.S. News & World Report*, as well as earning him several awards, including a Webby and a National Circle of Excellence Award through CASE.

Bart graduated magna cum laude from Anderson University, is a member of the Council for Advancement and Support of Education (CASE), has served as president of the Anderson

University Alumni Council, is a Senior Fellow at the Association for Biblical Higher Education (ABHE), is part of the Teaching Faculty for the NACCAP Leadership Development for Enrollment Professionals (LDEP), and is a contributing writer for Forbes.com. He is a frequent podcast guest and is often asked to speak at institutions and conferences on topics related to generative artificial intelligence, enrollment marketing, and website design.

If you would like to contact Bart, you can contact him directly at caylor@caylor-solutions.com!

ABOUT THE COMPANIES

CAYLOR SOLUTIONS

Caylor Solutions is an Indianapolis based, virtual marketing agency serving education clients across the United States and beyond. Founded in 2011, Caylor Solutions prides itself in providing customized branding, design and marketing solutions for colleges, universities, K-12 schools and educational organizations with one goal in mind: to advance education.

Through a diverse and experienced team of project managers, strategists, designers, writers and developers, Caylor Solutions strives to create impact for its clients through the development of strategic communication materials for a wide array of branding and marketing initiatives, such as:

- Marketing Consulting and Coaching
- Enrollment and Communication Strategies
- Communication Flows
- Marketing Plan Development, Consulting and Execution
- Brand Strategy and Development
- Messaging Development, Strategy and Execution

- Website Design and Development
- Print and Digital Marketing Collateral Execution

Visit caylor-solutions.com for a complete list of capabilities and case studies.

THE HIGHER ED MARKETER

With a heart for connection and impact, The Higher Ed Marketer was established to invite collaboration and foster a cycle of learning among higher ed marketers through content that both empowers marketers and builds community.

What was once a standalone podcast, The Higher Ed Marketer, has organically grown into a broad, knowledge-sharing entity for higher education and marketing professionals alike. Through various online resources, classes, books, the podcast and summits, The Higher Ed Marketer continues to highlight cutting-edge marketing tactics and inspire creative conversations.

Bart's love of learning and passion for innovative solutions have allowed him to dive head first into the world of Artificial Intelligence, particularly since the release of ChatGPT in late 2022. Through The Higher Ed Marketer, he leads the way in educating others and cultivating a community of learning in the ever evolving world of AI by hosting the first ever Virtual AI Summit.

The Higher Ed Marketer remains committed to learning, unlearning and relearning in order to bring valuable content, resources and inspiring information to audience members for years to come.

The Higher Ed Marketer Podcast:
- #1 on the Hannon Hill's "Must Listen Higher Ed Podcasts 2023"
- #4 on the Terminal Four's "Top 10 Podcasts of 2021 for Higher Ed Digital, Marketing, and Recruitment Teams"
- #7 on Olark's "Top 15 Ebooks & Podcasts for Higher Ed Enrollment Teams"
- #21 on Feedspot's "Best 50 Higher Education Podcasts"
- One of 4 higher ed podcast resources mentioned in Wiley's Recruiting and Retaining Adult Learners Journal September 2022 Issue
- Consistently ranked in the Top 100 of Apple marketing podcasts
- Three consecutive years running with over 150 episodes

Connect with us and view our current resources at thehigheredmarker.com.